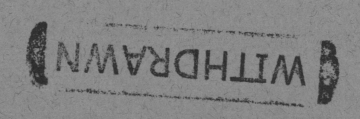

Wind rose that surrounded a compass, from the inside of the back cover of Battista Agnese's world atlas, Venezia, ca. 1544. Item no. 5.

Nautical Charts on Vellum
in the Library of Congress

Compiled by
Walter W. Ristow
and
R. A. Skelton

Library of Congress   Washington   1977

Library of Congress Cataloging in Publication Data

United States. Library of Congress.
   Nautical charts on vellum in the Library of Congress.

   Bibliography: p.
   Includes index.
   1. Nautical charts—Bibliography—Catalogs. 2. Maps, Manuscript—Bibliography—
Catalogs. 3. United States. Library of Congress. I. Ristow, Walter William, 1908–
II. Skelton, Raleigh Ashlin. III. Title.
Z6026.H9U66 1977 [GA361] 623.89'2   76-6923
ISBN 0-8444-0181-1

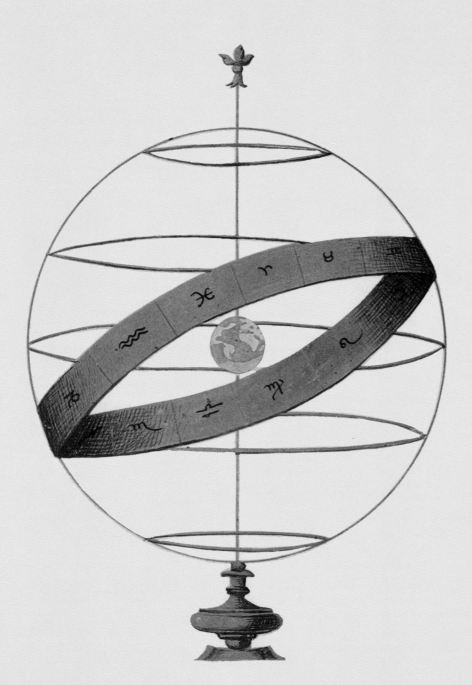

Preface

In 1961 R. A. (Peter) Skelton, then superintendent of the Map Room, British Museum, visited Washington, D.C. Supported by gift funds, Peter Skelton was employed by the Library of Congress, for a period of three weeks, to identify and prepare brief descriptions of the small collection of portolan charts and atlases preserved in the Geography and Map Division. During his brief incumbency, Skelton prepared preliminary descriptions of 17 charts and atlases, copies of which were subsequently filed with the respective items.

In November 1964, after Skelton's notes were reviewed, a letter was dispatched inquiring whether he might be able to edit and expand the preliminary descriptions submitted in 1961 and to describe several charts and atlases not included in the original survey. Skelton's reply was affirmative, subject to receipt of additional photocopies and to specified research, checking, and editing by specialists in the Geography and Map Division.

During the next year Skelton, occupied with several demanding research, writing, and lecture projects, was able to give only occasional attention to the portolan chart study. Nonetheless, on November 19, 1966, he wrote: "The catalog of your Portolan Charts is very nearly ready for printing and only needs checking on a few details before I send it to you. In fact, I may send it to you as it stands before Christmas so that you can see what remains to be done."

Skelton retired from his position in the British Museum early in 1967, with the expectation of spending more time on personal research and writing. In an April 18, 1967, letter to Arch C. Gerlach, then chief of the Geography and Map Division, Skelton wrote that retirement "will give an opportunity for pushing forward with a lot of work which I have had to neglect for want of time." In the same letter he affirmed that "one of the jobs which I have to complete as quickly as possible is the catalogue of your charts, which only needs a final revision before sending the copy."

Skelton's professional obligations, however, became even more pressing after his retirement, and the portolan chart list was laid aside for several years while he completed higher priority writing tasks. Relocation of the Library's Geography and Map Division to temporary facilities in Alexandria, Va., in September 1969 resulted in neglect of the project at this end. Several letters of inquiry were sent to Skelton during this period.

In reply to a March 23, 1970, letter Skelton wrote, "you have been

extremely patient about my descriptions of the L.C. charts and my slowness in preparing them for publication. Since receiving your letter I have revised them into not quite final form and enclose the first copy of those completed." He noted further that, "although (as I hope you will agree) the notices now seem to be in adequate form, you will observe that they still need some details for completion. I made no note of the colours, and perhaps you or one of your colleagues could add this to the notices; all measurements, whether of the charts or of scales, need checking and completion; and you may think that the bibliographical references are somewhat crudely expressed. I should be most grateful if you could arrange for these finishing touches to be applied."

Acknowledgment was sent to Skelton on April 8, 1970, with the assurance that "as time permits, and when your remaining notes are in, we will go over them, check measurements, add provenance data, reorder the numbering, and do final editing."

Skelton's next communication, dated November 20, 1970, reported, "I have had to lay aside temporarily the Catalogue of Portolan Charts, but hope to get it behind me round about Christmas. As you know, I have only two or three notices to complete, and the brief introductory essay on the Portolan Chart in general." This was the last letter from R. A. Skelton, for he died on December 7, 1970, as a result of injuries received in an automobile accident three days earlier.

In response to a February 4, 1971, letter, Mrs. Skelton wrote, on March 18, 1971, "I am sending you the portolan chart descriptions & also one or two reference notes that were in the file, but I have found no introductory essay so I am afraid this was never written. Peter [she continued] was always working against the clock and was forever having his own work interrupted by cries for help from other people—but it is very disappointing that he never completed his work for you."

During the past three and a half years, the cocompiler has, as time from other duties permitted, reviewed, supplemented, and edited Skelton's notes, compiled or completed descriptions for several portolan charts or atlases, and prepared the introductory essay.

In addition, an intensive search of the Geography and Map Division collections revealed additional nautical charts on vellum. Among these are a facsimile, on vellum, of the Catalan atlas of 1375 (no. 2), Samuel de Champlain's original 1607 manuscript chart of the coast of Nova Scotia (no. 15), an engraved chart on vellum of the North Atlantic (ca. 1660) by Pieter Goos (no. 18), and several 18-century charts prepared by staff members or students of the former Spanish Royal School of Navigation in Cadiz. Some of them (as is also true of several in the original list of 20) are not true portolan charts. The title for this catalog has, therefore, been changed to *Nautical Charts on Vellum in the Library of Congress.*

The Library's collection of nautical charts on vellum is a modest one. It includes, however, representative works of a number of the major schools of chartmakers. The collection, moreover, provides examples for studying the evolutionary development of navigation charts over a period of more than four centuries.

Charts on vellum were not among the earliest cartographic holdings of the Library of Congress. In fact, there was not a single example in the collections when a separate cartographic division was established in 1897, although the library held some 47,000 maps and 1,200 atlases at this time.

Philip Lee Phillips, first chief of the Library's Map Department, was an Americanist and a cartobibliographer. These two interests largely influenced his acquisitions policies, particularly in the earlier years of his tenure. During this period, portolan charts were apparently only of peripheral interest to him. In 1903, the Library purchased its first portolan-type chart, Lajonk and Siscara's *Descripcion de la Bahia de Santa Marta . . .* (no. 22). This representation of the coast of Florida conformed with Phillips' American interest. Significantly, the chart was not included among "noteworthy accessions" in the annual report of the division for fiscal years 1903 or 1904. Similarly, a 1678 Cavallini (no. 20) and John Thornton's 1681 chart (no. 21), acquired in 1904, were not mentioned in annual reports.

Among "noteworthy accessions" in the 1906 report were described "good examples of early cartographical work on vellum [including] a plan of Lima, Peru, in 1674, by Bernado Clemente [Bernardo Clemente Principe], and two portolanos. Of these, one, beautifully illuminated, is in two sheets bound in heavy wooden covers and signed 'Iouan Batta Cauullini fecit in ciuitate Liburni anno 1640' [no. 17]. This is primarily of the Mediterranean and bordering countries but also contains a curious inset drawing of the American continent. The other, a vellum bound portolano of the early part of the seventeenth century [actually mid-16th], composed of charts of Asia, Africa, the Mediterranean coasts, islands, etc., with 'Mare Oceano' and a sphere containing America, is the original colored chart on four sheets of vellum [no. 8]."

Phillips' report for fiscal year 1908 (July 1907-June 1908) reported the purchases of Bremond's 1670 portolan atlas (no. 19), and Sardi's 1802 manuscript copy, on vellum, of the 1367 Pizzigani chart. A manuscript chart of the Florida Keys (no. 30), prepared by Capt. David Cutler Braddock in 1756, was purchased in 1909. In 1910 the Library received, in the Henry Harrisse bequest, several rare cartographic items, among

them Samuel de Champlain's 1607 chart of the northeast coast of North America (no. 15). This distinctive item is not mentioned in the annual reports for 1910 or 1911, and it is possible that the Harrisse maps and charts were not transferred to the Map Division, from the Rare Book Division (where the major part of the Harrisse materials are preserved), until a year or two later.

By 1911 Phillips was sufficiently interested in portolan charts to include four of them (nos. 8, 17, 19, 20) in an exhibit of some of the division's more distinctive treasures. This represented half of the portolan, and portolan-like, charts, on vellum, which the Library had acquired to that time.

When Mateo Prunes' 1559 portolan (no. 7) was purchased, Phillips described it in a lengthy paragraph, in his 1913 annual report: "Among the noteworthy accessions of the past year, the first to be mentioned on account of its rarity and exceptional interest, is a well preserved early manuscript portolan or chart of the coast of the Mediterranean Sea, the Atlantic Ocean, and the North Sea. The author and the date of this chart are given in the inscription found near the left-hand border: 'Mateus Prunes in ciuitate Majorica, anno 1559.'. . . As a geographical record of the second half of the sixteenth century [this chart] is of considerable importance and is a valuable addition to the collection of cartographical treasures preserved in this Division."

In his report for the succeeding year (1914) Phillips advanced the opinion that "the prototype of the nautical chart entitled Portolan or compass charts, should be made an interesting part of the collection. As yet, [he continued] the Library has only *five* which are not considered of great rarity." Included in Phillips' five examples, apparently, were the 1560 [Martines] (8), the 1559 Prunes (7), the 1640 Cavallini (17), the 1670 Bremond (19), and the 1678 Cavallini (20). Not mentioned were five additional charts on vellum then in the collections.

The limitations which World War I placed on the acquisitions program were noted by Phillips in his 1915 report. Nonetheless, this proved to be one of the most productive years for portolan charts, with six new acquisitions (nos. 3, 4, 6, 11, 12, 14). All were purchased from Ludwig Rosenthal's antiquarian establishment in Munich. Among them are several of the Library's earliest original portolan charts.

Two mid-18th-century portolan-type charts were acquired in 1920, both of which show portions of America. Sardinera's ca. 1750 drawing is of Rio de Plata and adjoining lands (no. 28), while Espinosa's chart (no. 32) shows a section of the Gulf and southeastern Atlantic coasts of the present United States.

Acquired by purchase, and noted in the annual report for 1921, were

copies of two additional portolan charts, Pascoal Roiz' 1633 chart of the Atlantic Ocean (no. 16) and Manoel Ferreira's mid-18th-century chart of the same ocean (no. 29). The collections were next augmented in 1924, when an anonymous 16th-century Italian chart of the Mediterranean Sea (no. 13) was acquired.

Between 1925 and 1928 the Library purchased from Maggs Bros., London, a number of manuscript plans and charts in several lots. They were, reportedly, drawn between 1712 and 1824 by instructors and students at the former Naval School in Cadiz, Spain. Among the purchases were several portolan-type charts on vellum. Acquired in 1925 was a 1734 chart of the South Pacific Ocean, signed by Antonio de Mattos (no. 27). Five vellum charts were included in the 1928 purchase from Maggs (nos. 23, 24, 25, 26, 32).

The division's only gift of manuscript charts on vellum was received in 1929 with the presentation, by Edward Harkness of New York, of two anonymous 16th-century portolan charts of the Pacific coasts of Central and South America (nos. 9 and 10). "A 1764 plan of the Harbour of Pensacola in West-Florida" was purchased in 1934 from Francis Edward of London.

The Library's most distinctive and ornamental vellum item, the Agnese atlas, ca. 1544 (no. 5) was purchased in 1943. The only engraved chart on vellum in this catalog was purchased in 1949. It is Pieter Goos' *Paskaarte* of the North Atlantic and bordering portions of Europe and Africa, which was published around 1660 (no. 18). A facsimile on vellum of the Catalan Atlas, 1375, was purchased in 1960. It is the most recent addition to the Library's collection of nautical charts on vellum.

The 33 entries in this volume are arranged in chronological order. Facsimiles are arranged under the date of the original drawings, with the date of the reproduction shown in parentheses in the heading. Supplied dates are enclosed in brackets in the headings and in the description.

The form of the entries, in general, follows that used in *Catalogue des cartes nautiques sur vélin conservées au Département des cartes et plans* (Paris, Bibliothèque nationale, 1963), by Myriem Fonçin, Marcel Destombes, and Monique de la Roncière. Titles are given in the exact form and same spelling as found on the charts. For untitled charts, descriptive titles have been supplied, enclosed in brackets. Geographical names—except on original titles—accord with standards approved by the United States Board on Geographic Names.

WALTER W. RISTOW
Chief, Geography and Map Division
Library of Congress

Introduction

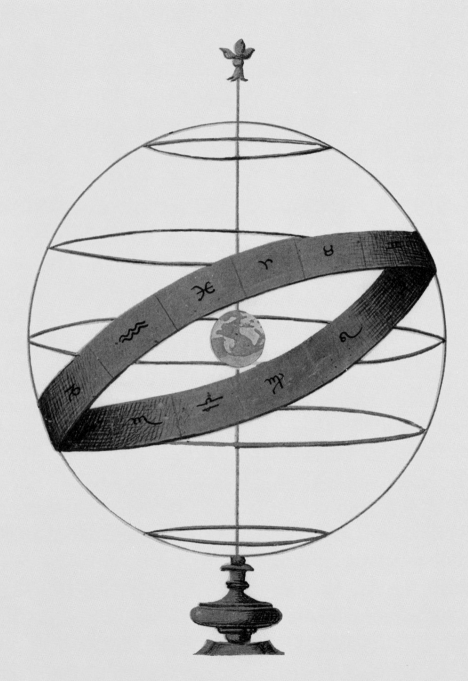

The distinction between charts and maps is not readily discernible. To define one term the dictionary must lean on the other, i.e., "a *chart* is a *map* intended for the use of navigators." Stressing the function of charts does, certainly, offer a criterion for differentiating them from maps. Simplistically, a map is most commonly looked at, or read, whereas a chart is used. Historically, charts were first employed in navigating the seas. More recently they have also guided aerial navigators and astronauts.

Because the safety of lives and possessions is dependent upon charts, their careful and accurate preparation has been a primary concern throughout the centuries. Scientific cartography, accordingly, owes much to medieval chartmakers who, responding to the needs and demands of seafarers in the 13th century, created practical and accurate navigation charts.

As Cortesão and Teixeiro da Moto (1960) have written, "a cartographic revolution occurred in the thirteenth century with the apparent sudden advent of a new type of chart, the so-called 'portolan-chart,' the origin of which is still not very clear. This coincided with the surge of seafaring activity and Atlantic exploration which began just before the end of that century, and was a consequence and a part of the great transformation through which Europe was passing." Portolan charts, they continue, "are indeed the first true charts in which medieval speculation and fantasy give place to scientific cartography based on experiment and observation, in accord with the spirit of the times. In fact they spring from the cultural revolution which took place in the thirteenth century."

The oldest extant portolan chart is undated but is believed to have been drawn between 1275 and 1300. Known as the Pisan Chart because it was discovered in Pisa, it probably also originated in that city. This chart, preserved in the Bibliothèque nationale, Paris, shows the Mediterranean and Black Seas as well as parts of western Europe and northwest Africa.

Because the earliest portolan charts are so well developed and complete, it is generally assumed that they evolved from older charts and sailing guides, known as portolanos. A fair number of portolan charts are preserved in various libraries and museums. Most numerous are 16th- and 17th-century works, but more than 130 charts dating from the 14th and 15th centuries have also survived.

Portolan charts, based as they were on direct observation utilizing

the mariner's compass, constituted a noteworthy improvement in cartography over the fanciful medieval scriptural maps. The charts in their earliest examples were limited to the Mediterranean and Black Seas and the Atlantic coasts of southwestern Europe. Oriented with north at the top, portolan charts depicted the coasts with a high degree of accuracy. The format and conventions established early in the development of portolan charts were closely adhered to for several centuries. Because of the relative uniformity of medieval navigation charts, Nordenskiold postulated a "normal portolan chart."

There were two principal production areas for medieval charts, one in northern Italy centered on the cities of Ancona, Genoa, and Venice, and a second in the western Mediterranean focused on Majorca and Barcelona. Whether the Italian or Catalan portolan chart developed first is not determined. Bagrow and Skelton note that "clearly the geographical source-material was originally common to both, although by the end of the 13th century, or somewhat earlier, the formal evolution of the Italian maps had stopped, while the Catalan maps continued to develop." Italian portolan charts are generally limited to the Mediterranean Sea, while the Catalan charts, or maps, reach beyond the confines of this water body, with some extending east-west from Scandinavia to eastern Asia, and south to include part of Africa.

Despite the hazardous nature of sailing and the obvious intensive use that was made of navigation charts, a number of them, as we have seen, withstood the ravages of time. This is, in part at least, because portolan charts were drawn on single skins of parchment or vellum, or on rectangular sections of vellum bound in book format, with leather, wood, velvet, or vellum covers.

No projection was employed for portolan charts, and latitude scales were not added until the 16th century. There were no borders on most of the single sheet charts, with the manuscript drawing usually extending to the margins of the skin. In contrast with earlier cartographic works, portolan charts are oriented with north at the top of the skin, an obvious adaptation to the use of the magnetic compass. This north orientation set the pattern for subsequent maps and charts. Although each chart was individually drawn and no two are identical, all appear to have been derived from a common original, i.e., Nordenskiold's "normal portolan."

Coastlines are shown with considerable detail and accuracy. Small islands and coastal relief features are exaggerated to emphasize their importance as landmarks. Bright colors—gold, red, blue, for example—are also used on some charts to give islands more prominence. River mouths are indicated, but the upper courses of streams and other interior geographical features are omitted. Offshore rocks and shoals are marked with dots or crosses.

There are, on portolan charts, numerous place names, which are in most instances lettered perpendicular to and inland from the shoreline. Lowercase letters are most commonly used for city names and uppercase for regional names. Lettering for most names is in black ink, with red ink used to identify places with special significance, such as a source of water or supplies, good anchorage, and so on. On later charts, selected cities are ornamented with flags, banners, or coats of arms. Miniature paintings decorate some charts. The Red Sea is generally colored a reddish-brown, and, in some instances, larger seas and oceans are portrayed with waving blue or green lines.

The most characteristic feature of portolan charts is the system of intersecting loxodromes, or rhumb lines, which crisscross each chart. Generally, 16 or 32 lines radiate from points in the various parts of the Mediterranean Sea. One common arrangement features a central rose, surrounded by several interconnecting secondary roses, which form points of an octagon. All the lines extend to the edge of the skin. Pilots could determine the relative positions of places and reckon their courses by utilizing the loxodrome network. On later charts the centers are ornamented, colored compass roses. To forestall possible error in reading, the lines were colored in a systematic pattern. The eight principal winds were drawn in black ink, green identified the eight half winds, and the 16 quarter winds were colored red. Some lines are in gold on charts in the more luxurious portolan atlases.

There is disagreement among authorities as to whether the system of loxodromes was drawn on the chart before or after the geographical features were set down. The most prevalent view, however, accords with Nordenskiold's observation, after examination of a number of charts, that the "portolan-network has been laid down after the drawing of the map itself."

Later charts include illustrations that are purely decorative, depicting such subjects as the Virgin and Child, Calvary with empty crosses, sailing ships—some engaged in deadly combat—and rulers seated upon thrones. There are cherub wind faces around the borders on some portolan charts and atlases.

All portolan charts have one or more graphical scales, which are frequently drawn on ribbons or scrolls and divided into fifths. The scales are often carelessly drafted in contrast with the accuracy and detail of other features on the charts. The unit of measurement employed is not known. Nordenskiold believed different units of measurement were used for the Mediterranean and Atlantic portions of the charts.

Embellished chart of the Mediterranean and western Europe, by Mateo Prunes, Majorca, 1559. Item no. 7.

Portolan charts are generally untitled and without legends. Many are unsigned and undated. As noted, however, techniques and conventions utilized were quite standardized over several centuries, and some continue to be used on modern nautical charts.

Some of the more decorative and elaborately embellished charts may never have gone to sea and were most likely prepared to brighten the walls and enrich private libraries of princes or wealthy tradesmen. This certainly was true of the manuscript atlases which were prepared during the 16th and 17th centuries. Production of portolan atlases reached maximum development during the middle of the 16th century in northern Italy. Battista Agnese, a native of Genoa who worked in Venice, and his associates were responsible for a large number of exquisitely drawn and illuminated manuscript atlases between about 1530 and 1564. More than 70 Agnese volumes are preserved in various libraries and archives. Later editions of Agnese atlases include maps which record the expansion of exploration on the American continents.

Italian portolan chartmakers limited their efforts to the Mediterranean Sea. Catalan charts embraced the Atlantic coasts of Europe and Africa and subsequently were expanded to encompass the new discoveries of the late 15th and 16th centuries. The Juan de la Cosa planisphere of 1500, the first to show the discoveries of Christopher Columbus in the new world, is in fact a portolan-type chart.

It is interesting to recall that manuscript charts on vellum continued to be favored by some navigators long after the invention of printing. Several vellum charts in the collections of the Geography and Map Division date from the latter half of the 18th century.

Printed sea atlases, however, were introduced toward the end of the 16th century and gradually gained adherents during the next two centuries. In the 19th century various countries established official charting offices and agencies, which have since been responsible for surveying and charting the oceans, seas, and harbors, and compiling and publishing accurate and up-to-date nautical charts. The efforts of the several official charting agencies are now coordinated through the International Hydrographic Bureau, which maintains offices in Monte Carlo, in the Principality of Monaco.

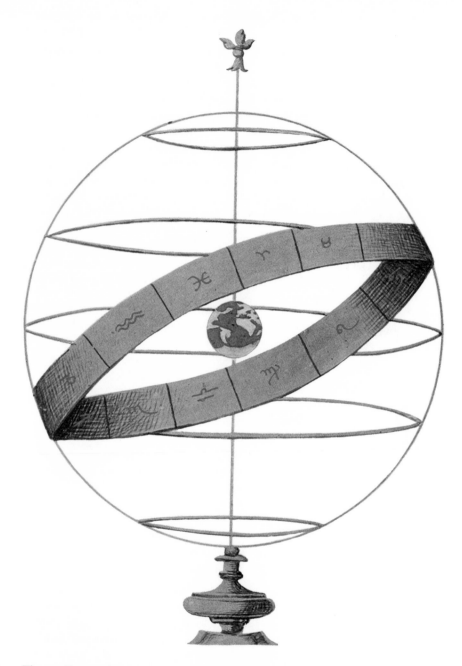

Catalog
of
Nautical Charts

The motif appearing on pages v, ix, 1, and 29 is a depiction of an armillary sphere from Battista Agnese's world atlas, Venezia, ca. 1544. Item no. 5.

1

Mediterranean Sea. Venezia, 1367 (Parma, 1802). Francesco and Marco Pizigano.

[Chart of the Mediterranean, with the Black and Caspian Seas, and the coasts of northwest Africa and western Europe, with the British Isles and part of Scandinavia] Drawn on two sheets of vellum, joined and cut to a rectangle 93 x 136 cm. Size within margins 86.5 x 128 cm. Manuscript, lightly colored. Copy by Agostinho Sardi, Parma, Italy, 1802.

The original Pizigano chart, made at Venezia in 1367 and preserved in the Biblioteca Palatina, Parma, Italy, is one of the earliest nautical charts, drawn in portolan style, to give details of the interiors of the countries represented and to delineate northern Europe. It has frequently been described; reference may be made to the description (with extensive bibliography) by M. Longhena in *Atlanti e carte nautiche . . . conservati nella Biblioteca e nell'Archivio di Parma* (Parma, Italy, 1907), p. 5-16.

The copyist's signature on this 1802 copy reads: "Parmae Anno MDCCCII./Ex Archetypo in Rᵃ Bibliotheca jussa Ferdinandi I° effinixit et lineavit Augustinus Sardi."

The Sardi copy was purchased by the Library of Congress from F. M. Terquani in October 1907 at a reported price of 240 French francs. It is not known whether the Library's Sardi copy is unique or if other manuscript copies of the Pizigano chart were made in 1802 or prepared before or after this date.

2

World. [Majorca] 1375 [Barcelona, 1960]. Abraham Cresques.

[Atlas of Europe, northern Africa, and Asia] Hand-illuminated facsimile, on six vellum leaves, each 64.6 x 49 cm, mounted on thin panels of wood, each 66 x 52 cm, and assembled in a folio solander case. With a descriptive essay, in Spanish, on one sheet of paper, 63 x 50 cm, by Professors J. Vernet and David Romano of the University of Barcelona. Facsimile edition distributed by Porter-Libros, Barcelona, Spain, 1960.

The original upon which this facsimile is based, known as the *Catalan Atlas of Charles V,* is preserved in the Bibliothèque nationale, Paris. It was prepared, probably at Majorca around 1375, by Abraham Cresques, with the assistance of his son, Jafuda Cresques. Cortesão (1971) states that "this famous world map is indeed the most remarkable and finest monument of the Middle Ages." The original consists of six sheets of vellum, 48 x 62 cm, attached to folding thin wooden boards and joined together. The first two sheets contain various cosmographical and astrological diagrams and long legends. The remaining four sheets when placed side by side form a planisphere of the then-known world.

The Catalan atlas has been frequently described (see the International Geographical Union's *Rapport . . .* fasc. 1). A number of reproductions have been made of the atlas, the more noteworthy of which are listed in the above-mentioned *Rapport.* An extensive bibliography relating to the atlas is also included in the *Rapport* entry.

The Library of Congress' facsimile is lavishly colored by hand, with gold leaf embellishments. It appears to have been copied, possibly from a slightly reduced photographic reproduction, from the hand-drawn facsimile of the Catalan atlas which was published at Paris in 1841. The facsimile here described was purchased in 1960 from Porter-Libros, Barcelona, Spain, for 16,600 Spanish pesetas.

3

Mediterranean Sea. [Genoa? ca. 1320–50?] Anonymous.

[Chart of the Mediterranean and Black Seas, extending from the coast of Palestine to the Balearic Islands and east coast of Spain] Unsigned and undated. Vellum, cut to an irregular rectangle, 41.7 x 57.5 cm. Matted and mounted between sheets of transparent lucite, 56 x 76 cm, taped at the edges.

The chart is simply drawn in portolan style, without decoration. Borders of double lines are visible along the bottom and left sides. A graduated scale at the bottom, toward the right, has five complete divisions, each of five spaces (= 5.8 cm), and two incomplete. There are no wind roses. The system of wind rays is centered in the Aegean Sea. The lines are colored red or green. Venezia, the only place represented by a pictorial symbol, is shown with crenelated buildings on each side of a canal.

Islands are colored solidly in green or red. Names of important places are written in red, and all other places are in black ink.

In his note about this chart, Almagià (1952) considers that the nomenclature, which he transcribes, and some archaic geographical representations, e.g., of Italy and the Black Sea, point to its execution in the 14th rather than the 15th century. He suggests that, in spite of some non-Venetian orthographies, the prominence given to Venezia may indicate that it was drawn there.

After extensive comparison of portolan chart characteristics which evidence evolutionary changes, or point to the habits or language of the people who made them, James E. Kelley, Jr., has deduced that the chart is of western Mediterranean origin, perhaps Genoese but *not* (stress is his) Venetian, and probably from the period 1320–50. Mr. Kelley's findings are documented in his paper entitled "The Oldest Portolan Chart in the New World," presented at the annual meeting of the Society for the History of Discoveries held in Charleston, South Carolina, in November 1976.

This chart was purchased by the Library of Congress in 1914 from Ludwig Rosenthal, Munich, at a reported price of 1,000 German marks.

References: Rosenthal catalog, 1914, no. 18; De Ricci, 1935, no. 143; Almagià, 1952, no. 1.

4

Europe and Mediterranean. [Siena?] 1484. Arnaldo Domenech.

[A 15th-century guide to weights and measures for European and Mediterranean cities] Signed and dated. Vellum, neck at the top, 59.5 x 37.5 cm. Matted and mounted between sheets of transparent lucite, 76 x 51 cm, taped at the edges.

Long believed to be a schematic map or diagram which indicated distances between the principal mercantile towns of Europe and the Levant, this chart was properly identified by J. E. Kelley, Jr., in 1973 as a 15th-century guide to weights and measures. Specifically, the wall chart contains this information: the number of pounds or rottoli per cantar or quintal (hundred-weight units) at each of the 27 towns listed, the equivalent weights (for converting from one system to another) between pairs of towns—as indicated by lines connecting vignettes of the pair in question—and fractional lengths of certain standard unit measures in use—usually in connection with the cloth trade—at various named places. (Kelley, 1973).

The signature, written in Catalan across the neck reads: "Asiento present hordenat a payen Les Responsions/dels pezos e mezures delahun boch al altre de/tots los presents bochs nnomenats Los quals/son cap e regiment de la mercadoria hordenat/e fet mi arnaldo domenech disipulo petri/Rosell anno dnj Mccc. Lxxxiiij." Kelley translates this as: "Here in the present [chart], arranged by country [are] the equivalents of the weights and measures between one port and another of all the presented ports named, which are the principal regulated markets; arranged and made by me, Arnaldo Domenech, apprentice to Petri Rosell, 1484 A.D."

Adjacent to the colophon, on the neck, is a large perspective view of a walled city with the legend "Sena es la psent ciutat," suggesting that the chart was drawn at Siena. The chart proper is contained within a rectangular border of double-ruled lines. Here are vignettes of 27 of the principal mercantile towns, with a network of interconnecting lines. The cities are joined at their bases to their respective coats of arms. Drawings are placed schematically, in rows, and not according to their geographical locations. The names are written so as to be read with the neck at the top. The relative positions follow:

Anglatera	bruges	Auynyo	macela	Genua
monpaler	Toloza	calles	Serdenya	piza
perpinya	barzalona		Sisilia	Napolis
Tortoza	mallorques		Tunis	Venezia
Valencia				Contastinopoli
Siuilia		Rodes		Candia
Alexandria	Acra	domas	barut	Xipra

(No symbols accompany the names famagosta and nicosia.)

Within the circle surrounding each drawing is a statement of the local value of the quintal converted into rottoli (the standard Mediterranean unit of weight), ranging from 100, the normal figure, to 144 at Valencia and 150 at Genoa and Pisa. Between the places depicted are drawn rays which terminate in statements of comparative weights (within the outer circles) expressed in quintals and rottoli. Exceptionally, four rays, terminated by a secondary notation—outside the circle—at the latter place, connect Rhodes and Alexandria.

Domenech's conversion chart for local weights and measures appears to be the only recorded example of its kind. It obviously was not intended to be used as a geographical map or chart and it is, therefore, inappro-

priate to compare it with the few medieval cartographic works which indicate distances between stations or ports. Whether Domenech obtained his data from some merchant's handbook, such as Balducci Pegalotti's *Practica della Mercatura* (c. 1340), or from oral information picked up in countinghouses and from factors cannot be ascertained. The possible, if surprising, indication of Siena as the city where the diagram was drawn may be significant, since almost all the work of medieval chartmakers, including Domenech, was executed in seaports. Siena was not a port but a financial center, and it is reasonable to conjecture that such a conversion table might have been useful in its banking houses.

This is one of only two known works by the Catalan cartographer Arnaldo Domenech (or Domeneth). The other, a chart in the National Maritime Museum, Greenwich (G.230:19), was signed by him in Naples in 1486 with the same formula, i.e., as discipulus of Petrus Roselli. The latter's nationality (whether Italian or Catalan) has been the subject of controversy, in which Domenech's work has been cited, e.g., by H. Winter in *Imago Mundi*, no. 9 (1952), and G. Caraci in *Memoria Geografiche*, no. 5 (1959). That Domenech, undoubtedly a Catalan, worked in Italy exemplifies the cultural continuum of the western Mediterranean during the 15th century.

Apart from a summary description by Uzielli in 1935 and brief references by De Ricci in 1935 and by Rey Pastor and Garcia Camarero in 1960, Domenech's chart was virtually unnoticed by students until J. E. Kelley, Jr., made a detailed study of it in 1973. It has never been reproduced.

In 1882 the vellum was in the possession of the Marchese Gerolamo di Colloredo. It was purchased by the Library of Congress in 1914, from Ludwig Rosenthal of Munich. The price was 1,500 German marks.

References: Uzielli and Amat de S. Filippo, 1882, no. 396; Rosenthal cat., 1914, no. 18; De Ricci, 1935, no. 142; Rey Pastor and Garcia Camarero, 1960, p. 84; Kelley, 1973.

5

World. Venezia, ca. 1544. Battista Agnese.

[Portolan atlas. Venezia, ca. 1544] 15 leaves, incl. 10 col. maps. 26 x 18 cm. Illuminated manuscript on vellum, in gold leaf and colors. Contemporary brown leather-tooled binding, stamped in gold. The four metal clasps it had originally are wanting. Binder's title: "Seecharten." Described as item 5914 in v. 5, *List of Geographical Atlases in the Library of Congress* (1958). Collation: recto of 1. [1] blank.— REVERENDISSIMUS I / CHRISTO PATER DNS / HIERONIMUS RVFFAVLT / ABBAS SACTI VEDASTI / ET SANCTI ADRIANI / in gold and red cartouche, verso of 1. [1]—coat of arms of Ruffault, recto of 1. [2] declination tables in three columns, verso of leaf [2]—armillary sphere, recto of leaf [3] —zodiac with a small Atlantic Hemisphere in the center, verso of leaf [3]—recto of leaf [4]—10 maps, verso of leaf [4]—recto of leaf [13]—verso of leaf [14-15] blank.

Inside the front cover is a notation in a modern hand: "Abt Hieron. Ruffault zu S. Vaast in Arras 1537 +1563 an der Spitze jenes niederland. Benedictiner Klosters." On the inside of the back cover there is a compass, with the needle lacking, surrounded by a wind rose in color.

Maps 1, 2, and 10 show America. No. 1 shows the Gulf of California which Ulloa discovered in 1539. On the same map Yucatan is shown as an island, and the east and west coasts of South America are only partially shown. On no. 2, the east coasts of North and South America are shown in their entirety and the west coasts only partially. Clumps of trees in green and gold are shown on no. 1, near the Moluccas, and on no. 2, in the Brazilian region of South America. The oval world map (no. 10) shows Magellan's route around the world and a route from Spain to Peru. The 12 wind cherubs on this map are named.

Henry R. Wagner (1931 and 1947) described 71 known examples of Agnese atlases, of which this is no. 33 (p. 75). He divides them into three types, namely, 1) Pre-Californian, 1535?-1542; 2) Post-Californian, 1542-1552?; and 3) 1552-1564; and he places the Library's copy in the second group.

Nothing is known about the chartmaker, Battista Agnese, apart from information appearing on his works, namely that he was Genoese and that he flourished at Venezia between 1536 and 1564. Leo Bagrow, in reviewing Wagner's bibliography in *Petermanns Mitteilungen*, v. 78, 1932, p. 190-191, indicates that it might be more correct to focus on the "Firma R. Agnese," which may have been active as early as 1514 and as late as 1597. Some 71 Agnese atlases, containing an average of 10 maps or charts, are known. Agnese may have made as many as 100 atlases in addition to a number of separate portolan charts.

Agnese's charts, including those in this atlas, are beautifully executed on vellum and illuminated in clear colors as well as with silver and gold. Their exquisite beauty is in keeping with the fact that they were made for Venetian merchant princes and ranking officials.

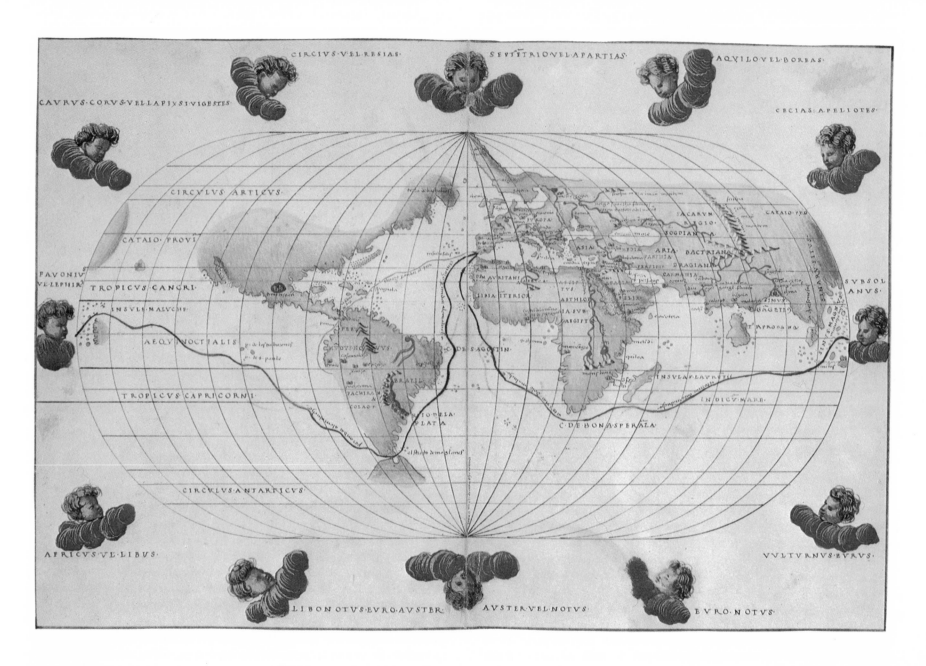

World map from Battista Agnese's atlas, Venezia, ca. 1544. Item no. 5.

Originally prepared for the Abbot of St. Vaast at Arras, this volume is known to have been in the library at Wernigerode in 1916, subsequently to have been offered for sale by Otto Lange in Florence, and to have been in the possession of Lathrop Harper in New York. It was acquired by the Library of Congress in 1943 for $8,250.

References: Winsor, 1897; Rüge, 1916; Wagner, 1931 and 1947; Martin and Ristow (*A la Carte*), 1972; Howse and Sanderson, 1973.

6

Mediterranean and western Europe. Marseille, 1550. Jaume Olives.

[Chart of the Mediterranean, the Black Sea, the coasts of western Europe and North America, with Madeira and the Canary Islands and part of the Baltic Sea] Signed and dated. Vellum, neck to the west. 57 x 79 cm. Slightly waterstained. Matted and mounted between sheets of transparent lucite, 76 x 101.5 cm, bolted at the edges.

The signature, written in Catalan on the neck, reads: "Jaume Ollives mallorqui / en marsela 1550." The chart, in portolan style, has its system of wind roses centered in the Tyrrhenian Sea, east of Sardinia. There are six decorative 32-point wind roses, including a very large one (with a fleur-de-lis as a north-indicator) drawn in the neck. Between this wind rose and the signature there is a drawing of the Virgin and Child. There are four scales, two in the top margin and two in the bottom, with five-space (9-mm) divisions.

The chart is lavishly decorated and colored—in the style typical of this Majorcan cartographer—with flags, pictures of cities, and representations of kings. To the north it embraces the southern part of Scandinavia and the Baltic Sea. North of Ireland, in the top left corner and bisected by the edge of the vellum, is a large island named Estilanda (cf. no. 7). In Africa the Atlas Mountains are pictorially delineated, and the west African coast extends as far south as the Ouro River. The Red Sea is shown, with red wavy lines, in the eastern part of the chart.

This is the earliest dated work of Jaume (or Jaime) Olives (fl. 1550-1565), the progenitor of a dynasty of Majorcan cartographers active in Italy and southern France until the end of the 17th century. Charts of Jaume Olives are signed from Marseille (1550, 1566), Majorca (1552), Messina (1553-1561), and Naples (1563).

Purchased from Ludwig Rosenthal, Munich, in 1914, for 2,000 German marks.

References: Rosenthal cat., 1914, no. 18; De Ricci, 1935, no. 145; Rey Pastor and García Camarero, p. 120.

7

Mediterranean and western Europe. Majorca, 1559. Mateo Prunes.

[Chart of the Mediterranean, the Black Sea, the coasts of western Europe and northwest Africa—with Madeira, the Canary Islands, the Azores and islands in the north Atlantic—and the Baltic Sea] Signed and dated. Vellum, neck to the west. 66 x 97 cm. Matted and mounted between sheets of transparent lucite, 81.5 x 113.7 cm, bolted at the edges. The signature, written in the neck in Latin, reads: "Mateus prunes In civitate majorica anno 1559."

The chart, in portolan style, has its system of wind roses centered in the Tyrrhenian Sea, east of Sardinia. Of the five decorative 32-point wind roses, three are larger and of more elaborate design. Eight wind heads, identified with names, are drawn at the edges of the vellum. Scrolls at the top and bottom of the skin contain distance scales, with five-space divisions (five spaces=8.5 mm). The chart is highly decorated, with bold pictorial representations of cities with banners and with portraits of kings. To decorate Africa there are drawings of animals, among them a giraffe, a unicorn, camels, elephants, and a stag. Continent names are framed within colored panels. On the neck are pictures of a bishop, the Virgin and Child with cherubs overhead, and an angel.

On the west coast of Africa the chart extends as far south as Rio da zanaga (the Senegal). Part of the Red Sea is included at the east edge of the vellum. The Atlas Mountains are not shown. In the north, Scandinavia is drawn with a curved northern outline that terminates in a promontory northeast of Scotland, as in 15th-century world maps. The Baltic Sea has the shape of a sack. Representation of islands in the northwestern part of the chart is suggestive of that on 15th-century maps, a technique which became standardized in Catalan cartography of the following century. (Cf. Nils A.E. Nordenskiold, *Bidrag till Nordens*

äldste Kartografi (1892), pl. no. 5, 7, 8; and Axel Anthon Björnbo, *Cartographia Groenlandica* (1912), p. 125-126.)

The representation exactly parallels that in a 1586 chart by Prunes, in the Bibliothèque nationale, Paris (Nordenskiöld, *Bidrag,* pl. no. 8). The islands named are Estilanda, Illeranda, I. anconie, Gorlan . . . (tip only), Fixlanda (Iceland), Isola verde (rectangular, at the western edge of the chart), Isola de brazil, and Isola de maydi.

Mateo Prunes (fl. 1533-1594) was a member of a family of Majorcan cartographers, all of whose work is signed in Majorca. Purchased by the Library of Congress from Otto Harassowitz in 1913 (price not recorded).

References: De Ricci, 1935, no. 146; Rey Pastor and García Camerero, 1960, p. 96-97.

World, Europe, Mediterranean Sea. [*Messina? ca. 1560*] *Anonymous* [*Joan Martines*].

[Nautical atlas including five charts on vellum, bound in contempory vellum covers, tooled, with gold leaf ornamentation] 28.5 x 20.7 cm. Each sheet cut to a rectangle, 28 x 41 cm, except the world map, which is on a sheet of paper 20.5 x 27 cm. Contents: [1] Eastern Mediterranean, with Greece and the Archipelago and the Black Sea; slightly overlaps no. 2. [2] Central Mediterranean; slightly overlaps no. 1 and 3. [3] Western Europe and the British Isles; includes the coast of northwest Africa (as far south as "zales", the Balearic Islands, the entire coasts of Spain, Portugal, France, the Low Countries, Denmark, and the southwest coast of Scandinavia, with the British Isles, Orkneys, Shetlands, and "hoocal" (Rockall, northwest of Ireland). Drawings of three ships. Some latitudes: C. Wrath 61°, Land's End 51½°, C. Finisterre 44°, C. St. Vincent 37°. Slightly overlaps no. 2 [4] Northwest Africa; extends south a short distance beyond Cape Verde and includes the archipelagos of the Azores, Madeira, the Canary Islands, and the Cape Verde Islands. Illustrated with drawings of three ships. Some latitudes: Madeira 32°, C. Blanco 21°, C. Verde 14°. Slightly overlaps no. 3. [5] World map drawn on an oval projection (ratio of equatorial axis to polar axis=3:2). Meridians are drawn at 30-degree intervals; the only parallels shown are the equator, the tropics, and the polar circles. The cartographer joins North America with eastern Asia; north of 20° to 30° latitude land extends to both the left and right edges of the map, "India" being written—about 30° north—in both the east and west.

The five sheets are boldly drawn, with bright, clear colors. On each chart there is a thick red line inside the edge of the vellum. On the world map, rays are drawn from a centrally located wind rose. There are on each of the other four charts three or four wind roses (with fleur-de-lis north-indicators) of uniform size, as well as one or two smaller ones, and scales set in scrolls (five spaces=one cm). Charts 3 and 4 have latitude scales drawn in the Atlantic. The nomenclature is Italian.

Internal evidence strongly indicates that the cartographer is Joan Martines, who worked at Messina and Naples between 1556 and 1591. The four regional charts closely resemble signed works by him, both in content (geographical outlines, ascribed latitudes, selection and orthography of names) and in form (style of coastal drawing, scrollwork of the scales, design of wind roses, detail of ships). Charts 1, 2, 3, and 4 correspond exactly, in extension and layout, with those in a normal Martines atlas. Only the world map is unusual for Martines; he preferred the hemispheric form for world maps in his atlases, and in none of those recorded is there an oval world map. The content of the world map in this atlas, moreover, is archaic.

Joan Martines, probably of Majorcan—or perhaps of Spanish—origin, produced a number of charts and atlases, all signed from Messina except two dated at Naples in 1591. Rey Pastor and García Camarero (1960, p. 101-113) list 34 signed works by Martines and attribute to him an additional 16 anonymous works. They do not, however, make reference to this atlas. José Ibáñez Cerdá, in the "Prologo" to a 1973 facsimile edition of a 1587 atlas by Martines, lists nine charts and 18 atlases signed by Joan Martines and 14 unsigned works attributed to him. The Library of Congress' atlas is also lacking in this inventory. J. F. Guillén (*Imago Mundi,* no. 12, 1955) has made a comprehensive analysis of Martines' style. If the world map is really by Martines, this atlas should presumably be placed early in his career, perhaps ca. 1560, because in world maps of later date he showed North America and Asia separated by the Strait of Anian.

Purchased by the Library of Congress in 1905, from E. G. Allen & Son, Ltd. [London?], this atlas was included in a lot of 24 items for which the total purchase price was £ 65.

References: De Ricci, 1935, no. 150; Guillén y Tato, 1955, p. 107-126.

7

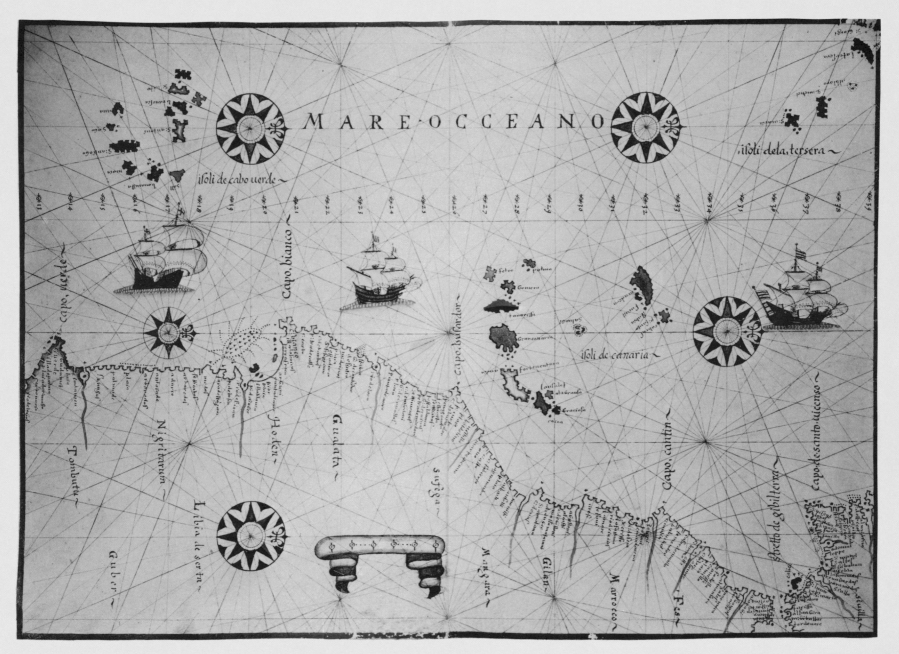

Chart of northwest Africa, including the Azores, Madeira, the Canary Islands, and the Cape Verde Islands. From an anonymous atlas, probably by Joan Martines, ca. 1560. Item no. 8.

9 & 10

Central and South America, Pacific Coast. [Spanish, 16th century] *Anonymous.*

[Two charts of the Pacific coasts of Central and South America (9) from Guatemala to northern Peru, with the Galapagos Islands; (10) from Mexico to northern Chile] Unsigned and undated. On vellum. No. 9, trimmed to a rough rectangle, 33.5 x 61.5 cm, matted and mounted between transparent lucite sheets, 51 x 75.8 cm, taped at the edges. No. 10, with neck to the south, 33 x 85 cm, matted and mounted between transparent lucite sheets, 76 x 100 cm, bolted at the edges.

Both charts have irregular areas cut, or torn, at the margins, as well as several holes. On each there are two double rows of pricked holes which extend across almost the full span of the skins and appear to have been made for thread or thongs. Their position and spacing, however, seem to exclude the possibility that they were used in binding a book. Although the two charts differ both in geographical delineation and in decorative design and appear to be the works of different cartographers, they seemingly share a common provenance and history and are, therefore, considered together.

No. 9 is drawn with the longer axis extending east and west. The wind roses (two complete and two incomplete) have fleur-de-lis north-indicators. The chart has a distance scale at the top right, partly torn away, each division measuring 3 mm, and a latitude scale, from 17° north to about 9° south with the bottom torn away. The abundant coastal nomenclature is carefully written, apparently in two different hands, both of the 16th century. Inland towns are marked by architectural drawings with flags. Three such towns are named—"qujto," "granada," and "leon." There are also drawings of large birds (Curassow?) and of a tree. No. 10, which is at about half the scale of no. 9, has a longer north-south axis. This chart is drawn in outline only, without names or legend; the coasts south of Punta de Aguja, Peru, are incorrectly oriented north northeast-south southwest, instead of north northwest-south southeast. By contrast, its technical and decorative elements are carefully finished. They include a scale of distances, on the neck, with divisions of four units (3 mm), a system of wind rays—with one large, elaborately designed wind rose and two smaller ones—drawings of two ships—one with a boat lowered—and an incomplete drawing of a third.

The apparently unfinished chart (no. 10) contains no evidence of date. The 1929 annual report of the Library of Congress Map Division notes that "it appears likely that [no. 9] was not made until after the year 1561 because it contains the place name *Landecho* for a village in Guatemala. This village seems to have been so designated for a president of the Audiencia of Guatemala, named Landecho, who assumed office in 1561."

Both charts were presented to the Library of Congress in 1929 by Edward S. Harkness of New York City.

Reference: De Ricci, 1935, no. 151, 152.

11

Mediterranean Sea, northwest Europe, northwest Africa. [Civita Vecchia? ca. 1590?] *Giacomo Scotto.*

[Portolan atlas, with eight charts on vellum, each 17 x 25 cm, within a double-ruled border, bound in a quarto volume in red velvet] Signed (on the chart of the Black Sea): "Jacobus Scottus Genouesi faciebat." Undated. Contents: [1] Northwest Europe, from Denmark to Brittany, and the British Isles. [2] Northwest Africa. [3] the Iberian Peninsula, with western France and the coast of Morocco. [4] Western Mediterranean. [5] Central Mediterranean, with Italy. [6 & 7] Eastern Mediterranean, from the Atlantic Ocean to Palestine. [8] Black Sea.

Each chart has an independent system of wind rays, which radiate outward from the centers, and separate scales (five spaces = 10 mm). The drawing is conventional, and the geographical delineation (of the British Isles, for example) is conservative, if not archaic. There is no iconography.

Giacomo Scotto was a Ligurian cartographer of Levento, near Genova, who was active toward the end of the 16th century. Two other works by him are known, dated from Civita Vecchia, respectively, 1589 and 1592 (Uzielli and Amat de S. Filippo, 1882, p. 156-157, 283).

The atlas was purchased by the Library of Congress in 1914, from Ludwig Rosenthal, Munich, for 3,000 German marks.

References: Rosenthal cat., 1914, no. 18; De Ricci, 1935, no. 147.

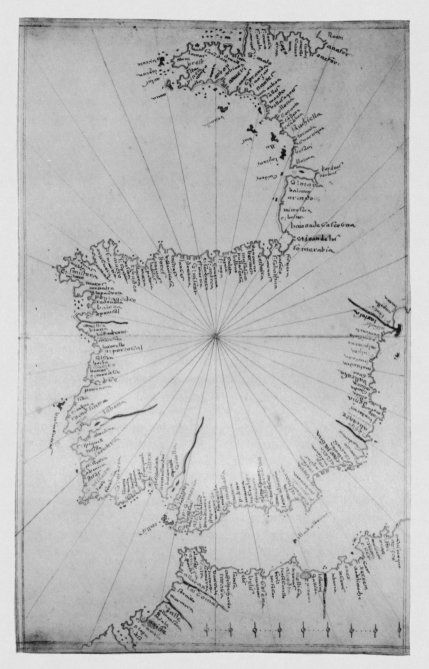

Iberian Peninsula. From a portolan atlas of the Mediterranean Sea, northwest Europe, and northwest Africa, by Giacomo Scotto. Item no. 11.

12

Mediterranean Sea. [Messina?] 16th century. Anonymous (Italian).

[Chart of the Mediterranean, the west coasts of Spain and France, and the northwest coast of Africa] Unsigned and undated. Vellum, trimmed to a narrow oblong, neck to the west, 19 x 50 cm. Matted and mounted between sheets of transparent lucite, 51 x 75.8 cm, taped at the edges.

The chart is framed in broad bands of color along the top and bottom, and around the neck. The center of the wind-rose system is in Sicily. There are 13 decorative wind roses (eight-pointed stars with fleur-de-lis north-indicators), including one in Spain and one in Portugal outside the main system. Within the neck there is a large 32-point wind rose, with a miniature of the Madonna and Child in the central roundel. In each corner there is a scale with five-unit divisions (five spaces = 7 mm). The nomenclature and style of decoration are Italian. The mannerist suggestion of the miniature in the neck points to a mid-16th-century date. J. A. Gere, of the Department of Prints and Drawings at the British Museum, suggests that its style, notably in the figure of the Child, suggests to an art historian the work of a local artist in Messina or Naples, executed under the influence of the Roman painter Polidoro da Caravaggio, who worked in those cities until his death about 1543. The geographical outlines, which have some affinity with those of later Messina cartographers such as Joan Martines, tend to support this hypothesis.

Purchased by the Library of Congress in 1914 from Ludwig Rosenthal, Munich, this chart cost 1,500 German marks.

References: Rosenthal cat., 1914, no. 18; De Ricci, 1935, no. 148.

13

Mediterranean Sea. 16th century. Anonymous (Italian).

[Chart of the Mediterranean, the Black Sea, and the coasts of western Europe and northwest Africa, with Madeira and the Canary Islands] Unsigned and undated. Vellum, cut to a rectangle, 54 x 77.5 cm.

Matted and mounted between sheets of transparent lucite, 76 x 101 cm, bolted at the edges.

The chart is drawn in portolan style and appears to have been cropped at the left, where a wind rose has been cut in half. Along the top and bottom edges, within a border of double lines, there are scales, each division of which has five units (5 mm). The system of wind roses is centered in Italy, to the north of Rome. There are four decorative wind roses, and half of a fifth, drawn in a style characteristically Italian—two, for example, have wedge-shaped north-indicators—and recalling the work of Vesconte Maggiolo, though the handwriting is not his. The nomenclature is Italian. In northwest Europe, the last two names on the chart are hanborg (Hamburg) and chitumer (Ditmarschen). The representation of Great Britain, with an undulatory strait or water feature separating England and Scotland, resembles that in the atlases of Battista Agnese, and the outline of Ireland is of a type which first appeared in the 16th century. (See M. C. Andrews, in *Proceedings* of the Society of Antiquaries of Scotland, 5th ser. v. 12, 1936, p. 18-19; and Belfast Natural History and Philosophical Society, *Proceedings and Reports*, 1923–1924.) On grounds of both content and decorative style it is impossible to accept De Ricci's dating of this chart to the 15th century, in which he presumably followed the Hamy and Baer catalogs.

The chart, which was earlier in the E. T. Hamy collection, was purchased by the Library of Congress in 1924 from Joseph Baer and Company, Zurich, for 1,500 Swiss francs.

References: Anderson Auction Co., *Portolan Charts . . . Collected by the Late Dr. . . . Hamy . . . To Be Sold by Auction . . . November 19, 1912*, no. 1 (with reproduction); Baer, sale catalog, 1924, no. 74; De Ricci, 1935, no. 144.

14

Mediterranean Sea. [Messina?] 16th century. Placido Oliva (?)

[Chart of the Mediterranean and Black Seas, with the west coast of Spain and Portugal] Signed. Vellum, neck to the west. 53.5 x 75.5 cm. Matted and mounted between sheets of transparent lucite, 76 x 101 cm, bolted at the edges.

The signature, in a cursive hand different than that of the nomenclature, was written vertically at the angle of the neck at the top, but most of it is wanting. The remaining segment reads: "Io placid. . . ." The chart is flamboyantly decorated in the characteristic style of the Oliva (Olives) family (see notes under no. 6, above). The wind-rose system, centered in the Tyrrhenian Sea, has four very large roses (with fleur-de-lis north-indicators) and 10 smaller ones. Distance scales at the top and bottom (5 units=1 cm) are set in scrolls. Pictorial features, gaily drawn and brightly colored, include bannered cities, a Calvary in the Holy Land, and real and imaginary animals—among them a unicorn, an elephant, an ostrich, and a dragon adjacent to the Red Sea.

A branch of the Oliva family, which settled at Messina between the last quarter of the 16th- and the third quarter of the 17th-century, assumed the name Caloiro et Oliva. One or more members of this family had the uncommon given name Placido. The fragmentary signature on this chart and the style of the design place the attribution beyond doubt. To which member of the family and to what date the chart is to be ascribed is less certain. Nordenskiöld (*Periplus*, p. 69) supposed that there was only one cartographer of this name working during the period 1615 to 1635. Rey Pastor and García Camarero (p. 132, 148-158), citing signed works between 1575 and 1665, however, think it necessary to postulate two—Placido Oliva (fl. 1575-1615) and Placido Caloiro et Oliva (fl. 1621-1665). Works of both are dated from Messina. It is to be noted, however, that all their known signatures are in Latin, whereas the signature on this chart appears to be in Italian. The style suggests the 16th rather than the 17th century, and the chart is accordingly ascribed to Placido Oliva.

It was purchased by the Library of Congress in 1914 from Ludwig Rosenthal, Munich, for 1,500 German marks.

References: Rosenthal cat., 1914, no. 18; De Ricci, 1935, no. 149.

15

NE Coast of North America. [France] 1607. Samuel de Champlain.

Descripsion des costs / pts, rades, Illes de la nouuele / france faict selon son vray / méridien. Avec la déclinaison de le ment / de plussieurs endrois selon que le / sieur de Castes le franc le démontre / en son liure de la mécométrie de l'em^{nt} / faict et observé par le

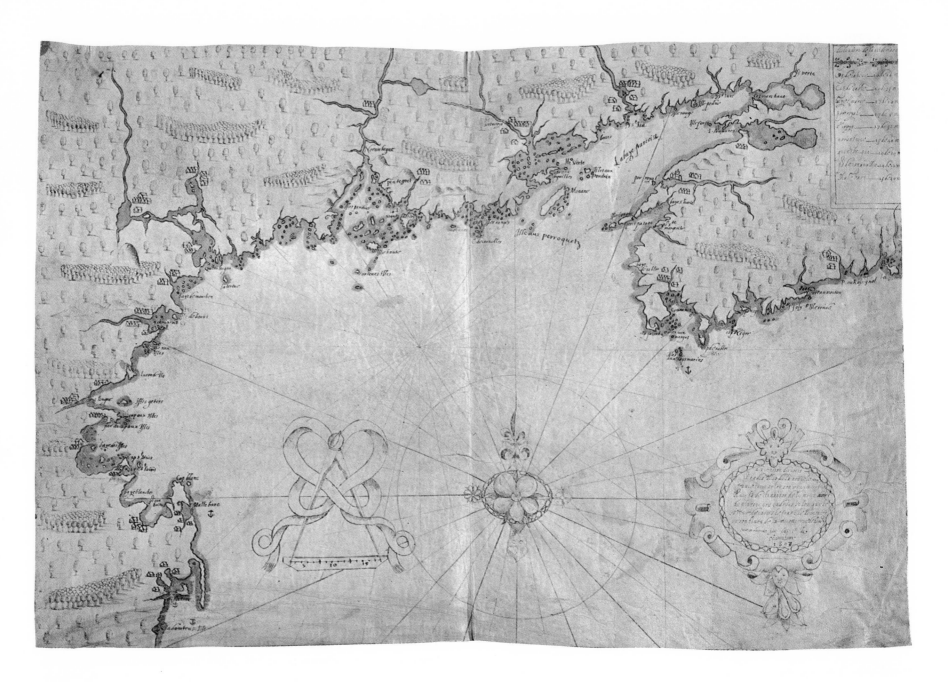

Northeast coast of North America, charted by Samuel de Champlain, 1607. Item no. 15.

sieur de / Champlain / 1607. Signed and dated. Manuscript on vellum, 37 x 54.5 cm. Outlines in brown ink, shorelines and major rivers tinted in green. Title cartouche in lower right corner, decorative scale in lower left quadrant. In the upper right corner there is a box, with longitudes for eight places, determined from Champlain's own calculations.

This map, personally executed by Champlain, ranks as one of the great cartographical treasures of America. It is the first delineation of this stretch of coast—from Cape Sable to south of Cape Cod—and was a principal source of Champlain's engraved map of 1612. Among places named are Port Royal, Frenchman's Bay, the offshore islands, and the St. Johns, St. Croix, Penobscot and Kennebec rivers.

From 1599 to 1601 Champlain went on an expedition to the West Indies under the auspices of the King of Spain. With a French party in 1603-1604, he explored the St. Lawrence River with Pontgravé and founded the St. Croix colony with De Monts. Champlain remained in Canada for three years during which time he explored and mapped the New England coast from Canso (Canceau) to Woods Hole. This chart was probably drawn by Champlain in the winter of 1606-1607. The legend, which appears to be in his handwriting, has the date 1606 corrected to 1607.

The chart has two systems of 32 rhumb lines, one of which radiates from a large compass rose, with a north-pointing fleur-de-lis, in the bottom center. To the northwest of the compass rose is a second set of lines, without a central rose, which overlaps and intersects the aforementioned system. A number of habitations dot the lengthy shore. Those of larger size perhaps identify the habitations of French settlers and the smaller huts may be Indian dwelling places. There are also many drawings of trees, singly and in groups, throughout the land portions of the chart. Place-names for the most part are written offshore and parallel with the top and bottom of the skin. A dotted line extending south from Port Royal, circling around the western end of Nova Scotia and continuing eastward to the edge of the chart, may indicate the route followed by ships from France to Port Royal.

Champlain's 1607 chart has been frequently described and reproduced in articles and books published over a long period of years. It came to the Library in 1910 with the bequest of Henry Harrisse, distinguished historian and author of *The Discovery of North America* and other significant works. It had earlier been owned by Gabriel Marcel.

References: Champlain; Ganong; Fite and Freeman, pl. no. 29; Baltimore, Museum of Art, *The World Encompassed*, no. 208.

16

Atlantic Ocean. Lisbõa, 1633. Pascoal Roiz.

[Chart of the Atlantic Ocean, the southeast Pacific Ocean, the southwest Indian Ocean, with the entire coasts of Africa and South America, Europe, and segments of North America and Asia] Signed and dated. Vellum, cut to a rough rectangle, 80 x 95 cm. Matted and mounted between sheets of transparent lucite, 96 x 114 cm, bolted at the edges.

The signature, within a scroll in the bottom right corner, reads: "Pascoal Roiz Afes In Lisboa. A VALENTIN PEREIRA." Below the scroll is the date: Anno De 1633. The system of wind roses (with 16 roses of various sizes) is centered northeast of Brazil. There are three distance scales at the bottom of the chart and one in Greenland (5 units = 3 mm) and latitude scales (10° = 64 mm) in the North and South Atlantic, offset from one another, with an oblique latitude scale off Newfoundland. The delineation of the lands and islands of the North Atlantic is archaic.

The chart is elaborately decorated with profuse ornamental and pictorial features, including a very large wind rose surmounted by a fleur-de-lis and a drawing of a pyx with the legend "Louuado Scia o Santissimo Sacremento" (bottom left); designs of "N.S. da Natevidade," the Crucifixion, Our Lady of the Conception, "Corpo Santo," and St. Anthony; Portuguese flags and standards, notably in South America and Africa; crosses in the Holy Land and Africa; scenes of African native life; and pictures of ships in the ocean, mainly along the bottom of the chart. The religious iconography in this, and in other contemporary Portuguese charts, is, as Professor Armando Cortesão has suggested, probably significant in a period when Portugal's maritime power was waning.

One other chart by Pascoal Roiz, dated 1632 and preserved at Dinant, France, is known. There is no additional information about this cartographer, although, as Captain Teixeira da Mota notes, many Portuguese pilots with the surname Roiz are mentioned in the records.

This chart was purchased from E. M. Terquem in 1920, for an undetermined price.

References: De Ricci, 1935, no. 153; D. Gernez, "Les cartes avec échelle de latitudes auxiliaire pour la région de Terre-Neuve," *Communications de l'Académie de Marine de Belgique,* 11 (1952), p. 113; Baltimore, Museum of Art, *The World Encompassed*, no. 107; Armando Cortesão

Chart of the Atlantic Ocean, by Pascoal Roiz, Lisbõa, 1633. Item no. 16.

and A. Teixeira da Mota, *Portugaliae Monumenta Cartographica,* v. 5 (1960), p. 21-22, and pl. no. 534.

17

Mediterranean Sea. Livorno, 1640. Giovanni Battista Cavallini.

[Two charts, half-joined at the backs and folded within oak board covers, 51 x 42 cm. a) The Mediterranean and part of the Black Sea, with insets of the east and west hemispheres; b) part of the eastern Mediterranean, with the Aegean Sea and Archipelago] Chart b, signed and dated, is drawn with west toward the top. Vellum, cut to rectangles, each 50 x 82 cm. The signature, at the top right corner of chart b, reads: "Jouan Batta Cavallini Fecit in Ciuitat Liburni Anno/1640."

Both charts are executed, illustrated, and colored in the florid style characteristic of the Oliva family and their later Italian followers. G. B. Cavallini was, perhaps, a pupil of Joan Oliva in Livorno (see below). Decorative elements common to both charts are the wind roses and the elaborate ornamental frames of the scales, of which each chart has three (in chart a, 5 units = 13 mm; in b, 5 units = 36 mm). Chart a also has scrolls which frame the names of continents; and pictures of cities with banners, mountains, palm trees, and a large Crucifixion—in southern Spain. The two hemispheres are drawn in the top and bottom left corners of chart a. The geographical content is archaic, being reminiscent of the last quarter of the 16th century. In a the wind-rose system is centered in Sicily, in b in the island of Naxos.

Giovanni Battista Cavallini was a Genoese cartographer by whom signed works are known dated from 1630 to 1669, all originating in Livorno. His charts carry on the tradition of the Oliva family, one of whose members, Joan (or Giovanni) Oliva, produced charts and atlases at Livorno from ca. 1620 to 1650, including two (in 1630 and 1636) signed jointly by him and G.B. Cavallini. Neither the pair of charts here described nor that described under no. 20 is in the published lists of Cavallini's work by Calegari (*Bolletino storico Livornese,* 1939, p. 200-205) and R. Almagià (*Rivista di Livorno,* 1958, p. 2-10).

Purchased by the Library of Congress in 1905, these charts were obtained from E. G. Allen & Son, Ltd., London, for £65.

References: Almagià, 1939; Calegari, 1958; Rey Pastor and García Camarero, 1960, p. 165.

18

Europe and North Atlantic. Amsterdam, ca. 1660. Pieter Goos.

Paskaarte Vertonende alle de Zekusten Europe Nieu/vez uytgegeven Door P. Goos. Amsterdam [1660] Vellum, trimmed to a rectangle, 72 x 91 cm. Nail holes along edges. Engraved chart, hand colored. Title cartouche at bottom center; imprint cartouche, near upper right corner, reads: Gedruckt t'Amsterdam Bij Pieter Goos Op't Water in de Vergulde Zee Spiegel. Scale cartouches in all four corners include Dutch, English, French, German, and Spanish scales of miles. The scale of the chart is 1:8,200,000 or approximately 125 miles to an inch.

The chart is oriented with west at the top. There are 16 systems of rhumb lines, two of which radiate from decorated and colored wind roses. Two other systems have half circles, decorated and colored, as their foci. Sailing ships are shown off the west coasts of Africa and Greenland, and there are drawings of two eskimos and two polar bears on Greenland. In north Africa there are representations of two elephants, and illustrations of two goats are shown in Scandinavia. The eastern extension of the Mediterranean Sea is an inset at the western edge of the chart, within the outlines of North Africa. Within the respective country boundaries there are decorative coats of arms for Barbary, Spain, France, Germany, England, Norway, Sweden, and Russia. There is but one coat of arms on the Iberian Peninsula and, because the dual monarchy was terminated in 1640, the chart is assumed to have been originally drawn before this date.

Pieter Goos was born in Amsterdam in 1616 and died there in 1675. He engraved and published a number of separate charts as well as two maritime atlases, which were issued in numerous editions between 1654 and 1688.

This chart by Goos is a redrawing of one which, according to Voorbeijtel Cannenburg (1948), "was published in the Low Countries from the end of the 16th to the middle of the 18th century and obviously was bought and used by Dutch sailors during not less than one century and a half." Voorbeijtel Cannenburg states that the earliest extant example is a manuscript chart by Cornelis Doetz, of Edam, now preserved in Berlin. The earliest extant printed version of the vellum chart was published in the early years of the 17th century by Willem Janszoon Blaeu. Credit is given to Doetz on the Blaeu engraving.

In an unpublished study James Welu, Worcester, Mass., Art Museum, has identified seven variants of the Paskaarte, all but one of which are, like the Library's Goos chart, printed on vellum. Few changes were made in the various versions of the chart throughout its long history. Voorbeijtel Cannenburg notes that "apparently the succeeding editors, without any twinges of conscience, copied the chart from their predecessors and often even the decoration remains the same."

The Goos chart was offered for sale by Maggs Brothers of London in their 1940 catalog no. 693 and reproduced as plates 16. The Library purchased it in 1949 from a dealer in Buenos Aires for $350.

Reference: Voorbeijtel Cannenburg, W. A Dutch chart that survived the ages. *Imago Mundi,* no. 4, 1948, p. 63.

19

Mediterranean Sea and western Europe. Marseille, 1670. Jean André Brémond.

[Atlas with five charts, on vellum, in contemporary full brown tooled leather binding, with gold leaf ornamentation and modern repairs on spine and edges] 49 x 35 cm. Signed and dated. Contents: 1. Carte particuliere de la Mer Mediterrané concistant an trois diversses fuilles 1670. 2. Partie de la Mer Mediterrannée 1670. 3. [Chart of the eastern Mediterranean and Aegean Seas]. 4. Carte particuliere de la Maier Mediterrannée contenant Du trois de Gibalta iusque Allexendrete 1670. 5. Carte particuliere de la Maier oceanne et partie de la Mediterrannée faicte a Marseille—par moy Jean Andre Bremond 1670. Vellum sheets cut to rectangles, each approximately 48.5 x 69 cm. Half of charts 1 and 5 are fastened respectively to the inside front and back covers, the other halves of these two charts and charts 2, 3, and 4 are mounted on four stiff boards to form the inner leaves of the atlas.

Charts 1, 2, and 3 show, respectively, at the same scale, the western, central, and eastern portions of the Mediterranean Sea, with some slight overlap. Chart 3 is drawn with east at the top. Chart 4 includes the full extent of the Mediterranean Sea, with adjacent European and African lands; and chart 5, oriented with west at the top, embraces northwest Africa, western Europe, the British Isles, and the eastern Atlantic Ocean. Charts 4 and 5 are at the same scale.

Each chart is bordered by a decorative colored frame, into which the geographical drawing extends in several instances. The scale on chart 1 is placed outside the frame, at the bottom. The charts are boldly drawn in portolan style with much crude baroque decoration, including figures of sovereigns, escutcheons, large fleur-de-lis, castles, Calvaries (in Palestine), and ships, or pairs of ships, in battle, the more skillful drawing of which suggests the work of a marine artist. Each chart has a single system of wind roses, with the rays extending over the entire surface. There are scales of nautical miles, in five-mile divisions (5 miles = 1 mm, or 2 mm) and, except chart 5, each has a scale of latitudes, numbered at degree intervals. Specimen latitudes are Alexandretta $39\frac{1}{2}°$, Gibraltar 37°, Finisterre 44°, Land's End 51°. The outlines of the coasts are drawn, with considerable detail, in portolan style. The copious nomenclature is written with care in an untutored formal hand, though (like the chart titles) with frequent phonetic eccentricities of orthography.

During the 17th century, hydrographic workshops at Marseilles were actively engaged in the production of manuscript charts. The earliest seem to be those of immigrant members of the Oliva, or Olives, family of Majorcan origin (see note to no. 6 above), working at Marseilles, intermittently at first (Jaume Oliva 1550, 1566; Joan Oliva 1613, 1614) but later permanently (Salvatori Oliva ca. 1619-1635; Francios Oliva ca. 1643-1662). Among the French hydrographers who, in a style derived from the Oliva family, charted the Mediterranean coasts during the first half of the century—with official encouragement from Colbert after about 1680—was Jean André Brémond. The workmanlike drawing and somewhat uneducated legends in his charts suggest the output of a seaman turned chartmaker.

The Library purchased this atlas in 1907, in Europe; but neither the seller nor purchase price are known.

Reference: De Ricci, 1935, no. 153a.

20

Mediterranean Sea. Livorno, 1678. Giovanni Battista Cavallini (?)

[Chart of the Mediterranean, the coast of Portugal, and the northwest coast of Africa] Signed and dated. Vellum, neck to the west.

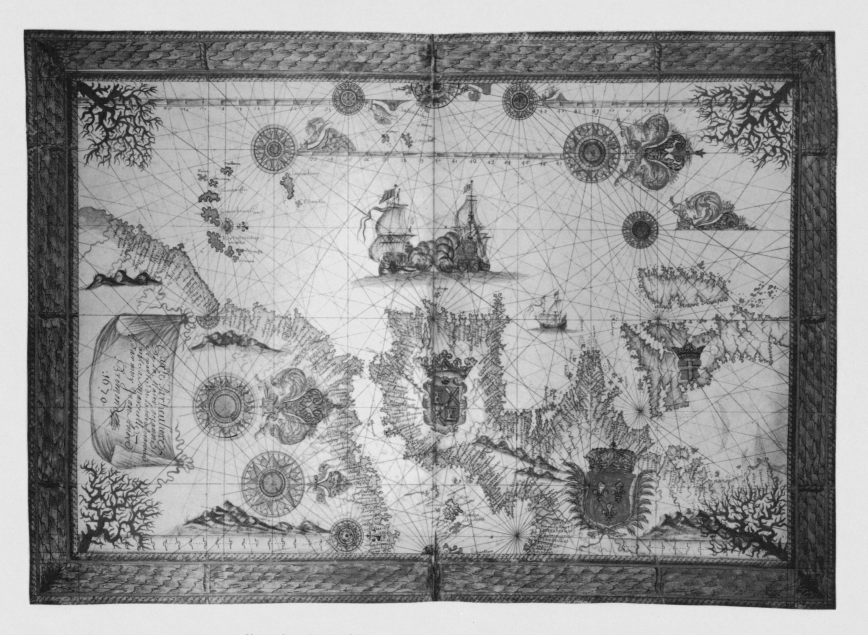

Chart of northwest Africa, western Europe, the British Isles, and the eastern Atlantic
Ocean. From Jean André Brémond's atlas, Marseille, 1670. Item no. 19.

21.5 x 47.5 cm. Matted and mounted between sheets of transparent lucite, 46 x 76 cm, taped at the edges.

The signature, across the neck, reads: "ill Cavallini in Liuorno/Anno 1678." Whether this refers to Giovanni Battista Cavallini—whose signed works are dated between 1630 and 1669—to his son Pietro—whose works span the period 1654 to 1669—or to the Cavallini workshop is uncertain. The chart is drawn and colored in a cruder and more flamboyant style than the chart of 1640 (no. 17). There are three distance scales (5 units=6 mm) along the top and bottom edges and a scale of latitudes across the neck. The profuse decorative elements which cover the map include cities, trees, mountain scenes, and scrollwork. Within a circular panel on the neck there is a painting of the cruifixion. There are 16 wind roses in three sizes, several with only semicircle centers, but all embellished and colored. The two largest wind roses are in the Aegean Sea and north Africa, with slightly smaller ones in Libya and Dalmatia. With the large number of wind roses and centers, the network of lines is quite dense. This chart is not recorded by Calegari or Almagia (see no. 17), nor by Rey Pastor and García Camarero.

Purchased by the Library of Congress in 1904 from Mr. W.P. Butter, Librarian, Forbes Library, Northampton, Massachusetts, for a reported price of $2.

Reference: De Ricci, 1935, no. 154.

21

South Atlantic Ocean. London, 1681. John Thornton.
[Chart of the South Atlantic Ocean, from 6°30′ N. to 40° S., with the coasts of Brazil and west Africa] Signed and dated. Vellum, cut to a rectangle 51.5 x 69 cm. Matted and mounted between sheets of transparent lucite, 76 x 101 cm, bolted at the edges.

In the bottom left portion is inscribed: "Made by John Thornton at the signe/of the Platt in the Minories/Anno Domj 1681." The solitary wind rose, surmounted by a fleur-de-lis, is centrally located on the chart. There is a scale of "Two Hundred English Leagues" (=112 mm), with 10-league divisions at the bottom and two latitude scales at the equator. The chart is drawn, colored, and lettered in the characteristic style of English nautical cartography during the latter half of the 17th century. A succession of chartmakers who worked "at the Signe of the Platt," including Nicholas Comberford (fl. 1616-1670), John Burston (fl. 1638-1663), and John Thornton (1641-1708), were recognized by E. García Camarero in *La Escuela cartográfica inglesa "at the Signe of the Platt,"* (1959). Thomas R. Smith and Tony Campbell have since established a chain of master-apprentice relationships in the Drapers Company, linking these men and others who practiced as makers of manuscript charts in a common style throughout the 17th century. Smith proposed the designation "The Thames School" for the group, while Campbell considers "Drapers' School" a more appropriate term. (T.R. Smith, "Nicholas Comberford, Seventeenth-century Chartmaker at the 'Signe of the Platt' in Ratcliff," [in press]; Tony Campbell, "The Drapers' Company and Its School of Seventeenth-Century Chart-makers," in *My Head Is a Map, Essays & Memoirs in Honour of R.V. Tooley* [London, 1973] edited by Helen Wallis and Sarah J. Tyacke.) Comberford was the master of Burston, to whom in turn Thornton was apprenticed in 1656, and became free in 1664.

T. R. Smith believes that this chart "is the last of six very similar representations beginning with Daniell, 1614 and 1637, and three by Comberford dated 1647, 1664 and 1670. They are all large charts on four wooden panels with very similar arrangement and area coverage that extends from English Channel in the Northeast, including the coasts of Europe and Africa, to the Cape. All charts show almost exactly this coverage with similar arrangement on horizontal panels and the rhumb network centered on West Africa ca. 7° N." Smith concludes that these charts were "used chiefly for voyages between the Cape and England, although obviously [they] would have been suitable for voyages to Brazil or the West Coast of Africa." The Library of Congress' 1681 Thornton, according to Smith, "is obviously a half chart showing only the two bottom panels but with identification definite because of Thornton's imprint in the lower left. . . . There are perhaps half a dozen of these 'half charts' among those which I have studied. The explanation is that four-panel mountings were cut in two across the middle, so [when] the panel became unhinged, charts became separated. . . . Another indication of the half chart . . . is the fact that [the one in the Library of Congress] has only a semicircle of eight secondary rhumb intersections instead of the sixteen for the full circle. The central intersection is top center on the chart." (Personal letter from T. R. Smith, dated April 11, 1974)

The chart was purchased in 1904 for $25 by the Library of Congress from Thury Baumgartner et Cie.

References: Campbell, 1973; De Ricci, 1935, 154a; García Camarero, 1959; Howse and Sanderson, 1973, p. 75; Smith (in press).

22

Florida coast. [Spain] 1700. Jaime Lajonk and Don Juan de Siscara.

Descripcion de la Bahia de Santa Maria de Galve, y Puerto de/Sⁿ Miguel de Panzacola con toda la Costa contigua y las demas Bahias que tiene en ella, hasta el Rio de/Apalache, observada, y reconozida por los Ingenieros Dⁿ Jaime Lajonk, y Don Juan de Siscara./1700/ Signed and dated. Manuscript chart on vellum, cut to a rectangle 51.5 x 68 cm.

The chart extends north-south from approximately 28°40' N. to 31°20' N. and east-west from approximately 85° E. to 87°45' E. It embraces the western segment of the panhandle of present Florida, extending from Pensacola to the mouth of the Apalachicola River. Centered below the title is a graphic scale beneath which is inscribed "Tronco de dies, y siete leguas, castellanos, con que se mide este Mapa." The fractional scale, reckoned from the distance between parallels, is approximately 1:665,000.

The chart is laid out on a rectangular grid with latitude readings on the right and left margins and longitude readings on the top and bottom margins. The chart is framed within a wide black border. A large decorative wind rose, with a north-pointing fleur-de-lis, is centered within the water area, with 32 lines radiating from it. Along the same parallel, at the east and west extremities of the chart, there are systems of radiating lines, with no wind roses. The coastline is accented with a gray-black wash, and there is an orange wash back from the coast. A number of names along the coast identify ports, bays, and rivers. Soundings are given for inland waters and bays. This chart is described, under WY248, in Woodbury Lowery's *A Descriptive List of Maps of the Spanish Possessions within the Present Limits of the United States, 1502-1820* (Washington, 1912), edited with notes by Philip Lee Phillips.

Purchased by the Library of Congress in 1903 for 600 pesetas from the collection of Pedro Vindel, this chart is described in his *Cátalogo ilustrado de obras Españolas* (Madrid), v. 3, 1903, title 2807.

Reference: Lowery, 1912.

23 & 24

Gulf of Mexico, West Indies, and Caribbean Sea. [Cadiz?] ca. 1730. Anonymous (Spanish).

[Two charts which together embrace the Gulf of Mexico and adjacent shores, the West Indies, including the Greater and Lesser Antilles, the Caribbean Sea, and the northern coast of South America] Manuscript charts on vellum, unsigned and undated.

Both charts are neatly drawn, in portolan style, with black ink, at the approximate scale of 1:4,000,000. The outlines of islands and the coastlines are skillfully executed and accentuated with gray shading. Shallow waters are marked with stippling. There are numerous place-names, most of which are written, portolan style, inland from the coast. On the eastern chart the name "Yᵃ Sⁿ Salvador" is applied to Eleuthera Island, directly east of Nassau in the Bahamas. Latitude readings on the left margins and longitude readings on the bottom margins, in degrees and minutes, are shown on both charts. Longitude is reckoned east from Tenerife.

Both charts are on sheets of vellum, with the edges trimmed to rectangles and with the neck protuberances at the top or north. They are laid out on rectangular grids which form part of the intricate systems of rhumb lines which radiate from a number of centers but include no wind roses.

The western chart (no. 23) measures 90 x 63.5 cm and the eastern chart (no. 24) is 97.5 x 64.5 cm. Near the lower left corner of no. 23 there is a table which lists 36 "Nombres delos Cayos de la Sonda dela Tortuga y parte del a Canal Vieja." A similar table in the neck of no. 24 lists 31 "Nombres de los Cayos dela Canal Vieja y Plazes de la Anguilla." Names in both tables are in black ink, with numerals in red ink. The names are indexed to corresponding numbers of keys off the north coast of Cuba and in the Florida Keys.

Both charts were included in a lot of material purchased by the Library, in January 1928, from Maggs Brothers of London. The several maps and charts had reportedly been executed or copied by staff or students of the Spanish Royal School of Navigation, Cadiz, during the early or mid-18th century.

25

Gulf of Mexico. [Cadiz?] ca. 1730. Anonymous (Spanish).

[Chart of the Gulf of Mexico and western portion of the Caribbean Sea, with adjoining coastal regions and islands] Manuscript chart on vellum, unsigned and undated. The edges have been neatly trimmed to form a five-sided polygon, 82 x 59.5 cm, with the neck protuberance at the top (north). Approximate scale 1:3,400,000.

The cartographic style and execution closely resembles that on charts 23 and 24, suggesting that they may be the works of the same chartmaker. This chart is also laid out on a rectangular projection which forms part of the rhumb-line systems. Chart 25 also has latitude readings on the left margin and longitude readings along the bottom—east of Tenerife. There are numerous names, neatly written, most of which read inland from the coast.

This chart, like numbers 23 and 24, was included in the purchase from Maggs Brothers in January 1928 and, like those charts, is ascribed to an anonymous student or staff member of the Spanish Royal School of Navigation, Cadiz.

26

Gulf of Mexico. [Cadiz?] ca. 1730. Anonymous (Spanish).

[Chart of the Gulf of Mexico and the western portion of the Caribbean Sea, with adjoining coastal regions and islands] Manuscript chart on vellum, unsigned and undated. The edges of the chart have been trimmed to form a five-sided polygon, 81 x 68 cm, with the neck protuberance at the top (north). Approximate scale 1:3,600,000.

The cartographic style and execution of this chart bear some resemblance to numbers 23, 24, and 25. The area covered is similar to that shown on number 23. The latitude and longitude readings on the left and bottom margins, respectively, also resemble those on charts 23, 24, and 25. The

rectangular grid and the rhumb line systems as well as the nomenclature are, likewise, similar.

This chart, which was also included in the January 1928 purchase from Maggs Brothers, is similarly ascribed to an anonymous student or staff member of the Spanish Royal School of Navigation.

27

South Pacific Ocean. San Lucar de Barrameda, 1734 (additions after 1741). Antonio de Mattos.

[Chart of the Pacific coasts of Central and South America and a portion of the Atlantic coast of Argentina, on Mercator projection] The title, within a decorative cartouche surmounted by the Spanish Royal arms, reads: Descripcion/o Carta Reducida, de los costas de Tierra/firma de la America Meridional, en la Mar del/Sur õ Pacifico Claculada [sic] la longitud Al Meri/diano de Tenerife y Corregido Algunos Yerros pr. lo que/Toca Al estrecho de Magallanes y el de Maire, y toda/la Tierra del Fuego, y las Islas al sur de la Tierra. Hecho en la ciudad de Sⁿ Lucar de/Barrameda por Antonio de/Mattos Año de/1734. Vellum, neck to the south, 124 x 73.5 cm.

The chart includes latitude and longitude lines, with readings on the margins. (One degree of latitude = 18 mm) A green marginal line frames the entire chart. The chart extends north to latitude 19° N., on the west coast of Mexico and south beyond Tierra del Fuego. The coastline of South America is continued northeast along the Atlantic shore of Argentina to latitude 30° S. There are no wind roses, but directional lines radiate outward from eight centers in the Pacific Ocean and from one in the Atlantic. There are numerous names along the coasts, including all major cities, as well as many small settlements. The coastline of South America has been completely redrawn, apparently after 1741.

Purchased in 1925 by the Library of Congress for £26. Seller not known, possibly Maggs Bros. of London.

28

Rio de la Plata, Argentina. [*Spain, ca. 1750*] *Sardinera.*

Nueba Descripcion/de el Gran Rio de la Plata Nuebmente, Corre/gido, de muchos Errores. Expresando Las/ˢlas Brazas que ay de Bajamar, ordinaxia/admirtiendo que enlas Mareas Grandes, que/suseden, conlos Vientos, Sur y sueste, Crese/El Agua, Algo Mas de Una Braza, yenlas/Mareas Ordinarias, Crese El Agua tres/quartro Piez./La Calidad, De el Fondo, Enlas Canales, Es/Lama Suelta, Enlos Bancos y Placeres, Es/Arena Parda y Dura Menos, Enlos siguientes/A. Lama y Conchuela/B. Arena Fina Megra/C. Barro Duro y Piedrecitas/D. Canal Del Sur Arena y Cascajo/Sardinera Fecit. Signed. Undated. Manuscript chart on vellum, elongated neck to the left, 52 x 97 cm. Colored. Scale ca. 1:950,000. Insets: (a) Plano Dela Encenada de/Barragan, situado Ala Ptte./Del Sur, En el Rio dela Plata/A. Riachuelo De Santiago/L. Canal de Santiago/P. Place ge seue de Bajamar/Q. Canal de lama suelta/R. Arena Blanca/S. Arena Negra/ (b) [Montevideo Harbor].

The main chart and the two insets are neatly and skillfully drawn. The right margin, divided into degrees of latitude, extends from 33°5' to 37°10' S., and the bottom margin is divided into a scale of 50 leagues (Escala de singuenta leguas De el Gran Rio de la Plata). Thirty-two directional lines radiate from each of two centers in the mouth of the Rio de la Plata. Both systems have half fleur-de-lis north-indicators. The eastern center is decorated with a red eight-pointed star. The two insets have networks with 16 directional lines radiating from undecorated centers. Both systems have, however, half fleur-de-lis north-indicators. There are numerous soundings in the waters on the main chart as well as on the insets. Major banks are delimited with dotted lines and accented with a yellow wash. On all three charts the coastline is traced in green. Trees, also colored green, are drawn along various portions of the coast, singly and in groups. Several prominent relief features are shown in profile, with gray and green washes. Cities and towns are colored red. On the Barragan inset, there are red-roofed drawings of some 15 edifices of varying sizes. The title of the main chart is set within a banner cartouche, located within the base of the neck. It is oriented with the left side of the skin. The cartouche is drawn as if suspended from a rope which is borne by a crudely executed winged cherub.

This chart was originally tentatively dated 1650?. The presence of "Puertto de S. Phelipe" (Montevideo) indicates, however, that it was drawn after 1726. Further, comparison with a 1719 manuscript chart of the same area shows the Sardinera chart to include more features and greater detail. A 1789 chart, however, is more complete and detailed than the Sardinera. The latter is, therefore, dated ca. 1750.

Several nail holes around the borders suggest that the chart may, at one time, have been fastened to a board. On the verso within the neck extension is written, in a contemporary hand, "Rio de la Plata."

In the neck area, in a modern hand, is the inscription "Phillipps MS. 26437." This number is also written on the verso, where there is affixed a circular label with the number "407." The Phillipps number indicates that the chart was formerly the property of Sir Thomas Phillipps, the renowned 19th-century British collector. The latter is the number of this item in the catalog for Sotheby's (London) sale of July 24-27, 1919. The Library purchased the Sardinera chart at this sale for £9, English.

29

Atlantic Ocean. Lisbõa, mid-18th century. Manoel Ferreira.

[Chart of the Atlantic Ocean, from 37° N. to 42° S.] Vellum, neck to the north, 83 x 61.5 cm. Matted and mounted between sheets of transparent lucite, 101 x 76 cm, bolted at the edges. The signature, in the lower right corner, reads: "Feita por Mᵉˡ Ferrᵃ Portugal."

The center of the system of wind roses is west of Sierra Leone. There are four decorative wind roses, all with fleur-de-lis north-indicators. At the top of the chart there is a large decorative fleur-de-lis. The equator is divided into single degrees (0°-45°, 319°-360°), with the prime meridian passing through Cape Verde. There are two latitude scales, offset at the equator. The scale of longitude at the equator is 10° to 65 mm, of latitude, 10° to 82 mm. The chart embraces western Europe with the British Isles, the western Mediterranean, the north, west, and south coasts of Africa, Brazil, and in the northwest, *Terra nova*. The chart is lavishly decorated and colored. There are Portuguese flags in Morocco, Angola, and Brazil, a Dutch flag at the Cape of Good Hope, and a large drawing of Mina.

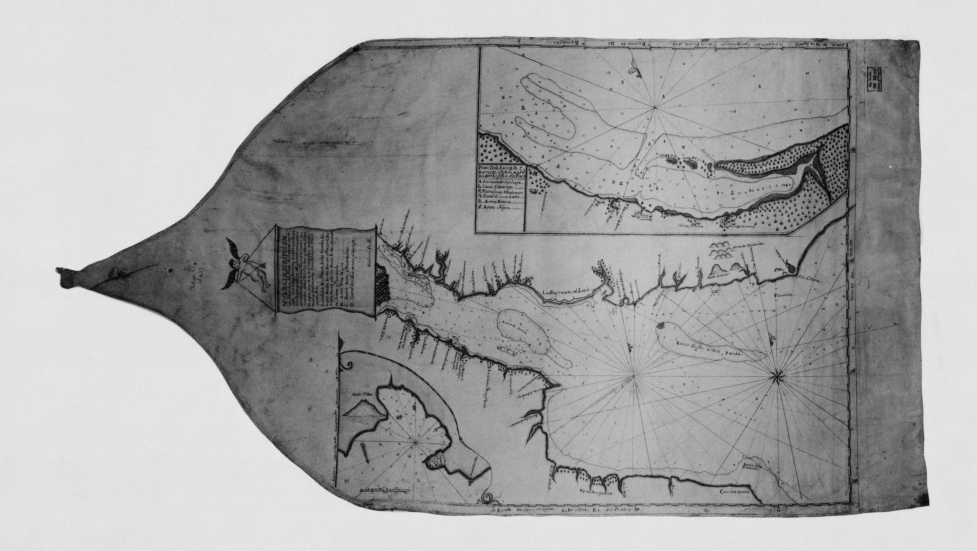

Mouth of the Rio de la Plata, Argentina. Item no. 28.

Other charts by Manoel Ferreira of Portugal are preserved in the Sociedade de Geografia at Lisbõa. One is dated 1764.

Acquired by the Library of Congress in 1921. Provenance unknown.

Reference: De Ricci, 1935, no. 155.

30

Florida Keys. Georgia (?), 1756. David Cutler Braddock.

The Coast of Florida from the dry Tortugas/To the old Cape by David Cutler Braddock 1756. Signed and dated. Drawn on sheet of vellum cut to a rectangle approximately 68.4 x 80.3 cm. Scale 25 cm equals 20 leagues (approximately 1:500,000).

The chart is drawn without a latitude-longitude grid and lacks marginal lines. It is oriented with south at the top. In the bottom center there is a north-pointing fleur-de-lis. There are two wind systems, one centered near the upper left corner southeast of Key François, the other in the upper center of the chart, almost directly north of Key West. Both systems have 24 solid directional lines and eight dotted lines. The intersecting points are not decorated with wind roses. Portions of the coast of Florida, the outlines of the Keys, and other features are accentuated in heavy black ink. The remainder of the Florida coast as well as soundings and text are in ink, which has faded to a greenish gray. Soundings are rather sparsely distributed over the chart. The title of the chart occupies space near the left center. It has no bordering frame or cartouche. Below the title are listed the names of 28 Florida Keys, which are keyed to numbers on the corresponding islands. Following the names of the Keys there is a lengthy manuscript inscription which gives detailed navigating directions for negotiating the waters around the Keys. There are briefer inscriptions in six other places on the chart which give additional sailing instructions, information about fishing, and notes indicating changes from the standard scale in two areas. On the verso of the vellum there is a lengthy note with information about sources for fresh water on the various Keys and a brief glossary with English and Spanish equivalents.

Little is known about David Cutler Braddock who prepared this interesting chart. He was, obviously, English in origin. Below the scale it is noted that "Capt Braddock 1756 in Company with four outher vessels from new Providence [Bahamas?] in a gale of wind ran into the Southermost Channels. . . ." An additional clue is given by Bernard Romans in *A Concise Natural History of East and West Florida* (University of Florida Press, 1962), a facsimile reproduction of the 1775 edition with introduction by Rembert W. Patrick. In directions to navigators, in the appendix to the volume, Romans writes that "The Harbour [of Tampa] is made by a range of islands lying before it, the southernmost of which is called Long-Island; its north end is called Grant's point, in honor of governor Grant; the next lying about a mile North of it, is called Pollux Key; another about 1¼ mile to the NW b N of that is named Castor Key, in honor of two privateers, one of which was commanded by the late Capt. Braddock of Georgia: these two vessels cruized in those seas about the year 1744 or 1745; and Capt. Braddock was generally acknowledged the first Englishman who explored this bay. I have seen his original draught which (considering the circumstances under which it was taken) was pretty exact." Romans was, seemingly, not familiar with Braddock's chart of the Keys. We have no record that the Tampa Bay chart is extant. Along the west coast of Florida on the chart of the Florida Keys here described it is noted that "the Spaniards told Capt. Braddock that Bay Carlos was a very good harbour but can say nothing of his own knowledge." Inasmuch as Tampa Bay is to the north of Bay Carlos, we may infer that Braddock's chart of the Keys predated his rendition of Tampa Bay, and that Romans' dating of the latter was some 10 or 12 years early.

Louis De Vorsey, of the University of Georgia, agrees "that Romans is indeed off by 10 or 12 years in his account of Braddock's survey of Tampa Bay." De Vorsey adds that "on December 10, 1756, [Braddock] was described as fitting out a 'Privateer Sloop' here in Georgia (*Col. Recs.*, VIII, p. 448). Chances are that he then sailed south to the Keys to execute the chart [of the Florida Keys] and then on to the west coast and Tampa." De Vorsey notes that "Braddock was a mariner who had large holdings on the Ogeechee River. There is a Braddock's Mill Creek to commemorate his residence in the area. He was also a member of Gorgia's colonial legislature representing Octon."

It will be recalled that the Spaniards were a considerable threat to the small and struggling British colony in Georgia. Only by good fortune and strategy was a major Spanish invasion threat thwarted in June and July 1742. Subsequently Governor Oglethorpe felt more confident to support attacks on Spanish settlements in Florida, to send out privateers to harass enemy shipping, and to survey the coasts and waters. Braddock's expedition possibly had Oglethorpe's support, or, at least, his blessing.

Captain Braddock's chart of the Florida Keys was purchased by the Library of Congress in 1909. In the summer of that year Philip Lee Phil-

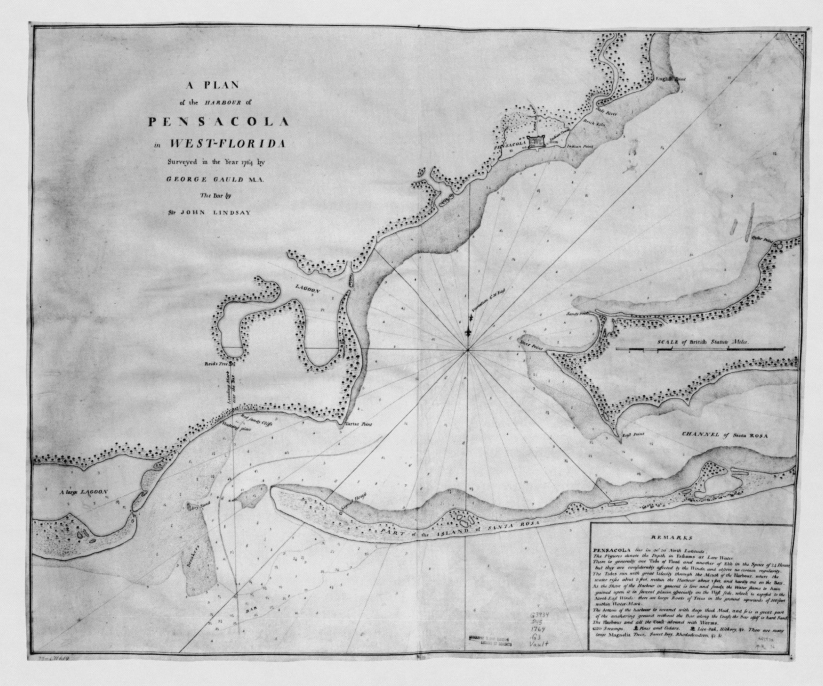

A PLAN
of the *HARBOUR* of
PENSACOLA
in *WEST-FLORIDA*
Surveyed in the Year 1764 by
GEORGE GAULD M.A.
The Bar by
Sir JOHN LINDSAY

Pensacola Harbour, Florida, 1764, by George Gauld and John Lindsay. Item no. 31.

lips, then chief of the Map Division, visited Europe on a procurement mission, and the Braddock item may have been among his accessions. Order Division records that the chart of the Florida Keys was purchased from Henry Stevens Sons & Stiles for £3.

References: Letter, dated April 7, 1975, from Louis De Vorsey, Dept. of Geography, University of Georgia.

31

Pensacola Harbour, Florida [*Pensacola, Florida*] *1764. George Gauld and John Lindsay.*

A Plan/of the Harbour of/Pensacola/in West-Florida/Surveyed in the Year 1764 by/George Gauld M.A./The Bar by/Sir John Lindsay. Drawn on sheet of vellum cut to a rectangle 56 × 70 cm. Within neat line, 55 × 69 cm. Approximate scale 1:32,500.

The chart is neatly executed and framed within a double-line border. In the lower right corner, within an 11 × 18 cm box, are "Remarks," which include the latitude of Pensacola, explanation of depth figures in fathoms, information about tides, winds, and composition of the harbor bottom, and symbols used for "Swamps," "Pines and Cedars," and "Live-Oak, Hickory, &c." The title, in the upper left corner, is without a frame or cartouche. A system of wind rays, in red ink, has its intersection near the center of the harbor. Just above the point of intersection, a small red fleur-de-lis points to the north. A slightly smaller fleur-de-lis, drawn in black ink, indicates a compass "Variation 4°30' East." Shorelines are in black ink over which there is superimposed a green wash. Bordering most sections of the coast and on portions of the Island of Santa Rosa, there are neat representations of trees and swamps. The city of Pensacola, enclosed within fortified walls, is colored red. Outside the fortifications there are several isolated structures, as well as an "Indian Town." The "Road to Mobile" extends north and northwest from the city. Centered on a peninsula, across the bay, to the southeast of Pensacola, there is a "Scale of British Statute Miles."

George Gauld, a foremost English hydrographic surveyor and chartmaker of the mid-18th century, was born in 1732 at Ardbrack, in the parish of Botriphny, in Bamfshire. He received his education at King's College, Aberdeen, following which he entered the British Naval Service. About the year 1759 Gauld is known to have served in the Mediterran-

ean on His Majesty's Ship the *Preston* under Commodore A. Forrest.

Following the Seven Years War, Britain gained possession of Florida. Notwithstanding several centuries of Spanish maritime activity in the Caribbean and Gulf of Mexico, charts of these waters and coasts were generally of inferior quality. The Lords Commissioners of the Admiralty, accordingly, resolved to have a detailed survey made of all the newly acquired lands and waters. George Gauld was appointed to conduct the hydrographic and coastal surveys. In March 1764 he embarked for Florida aboard the *Tartar,* under the command of Sir John Lindsay. After a stop in Jamaica, Lindsay, now appointed Commodore to command in the Gulf of Mexico, sailed the *Tartar* to Pensacola, the intended new capital of West Florida. From August 1764 until the end of 1771, Gauld conducted surveys of the coasts and harbors of West Florida and East Florida, the mouth of the Mississippi River, and the shores of the Gulf of Mexico. Subsequent to 1771 Gauld prepared surveys of Kingston Harbor, Jamaica, the Dry Tortugas, and the Florida Keys. A number of the resulting charts were subsequently published by William Faden, Geographer to the King. To accompany Gauld's charts, Faden published *An Account of The Surveys of Florida, &c. With Directions for Sailing From Jamaica or the West Indies.*

Gauld's *Plan of the Harbour of Pensacola* was apparently never published. An unsigned, untitled chart closely resembling Gauld's *Harbour of Pensacola* is preserved in the British Public Record Office, London. There is a photoreproduction of this chart in the Geography and Map Division, Library of Congress.

Purchased by the Library of Congress from Francis Edwards, London, in 1934, at a reported price of £ 8.

References: Gauld, 1790; Romans, 1775.

32

Caribbean, Gulf of Mexico, West Indies. Campeche, Mexico, 1765. Pedro A. Espinosa.

DESCRIPCION DE/las Costas Islas Placeres i Bajos delas/Indias Occidentales, Corregida i Calculada/al Meridiano dela Isla/DE THENERIPHE ENLAS/Canarias por/PEDRO ALCANTARA ESPINOSA/Campeche i/Abril 10 de 1765. Signed and dated. Drawn on a sheet of vellum cut to a five-sided polygon, with upper and lower margins

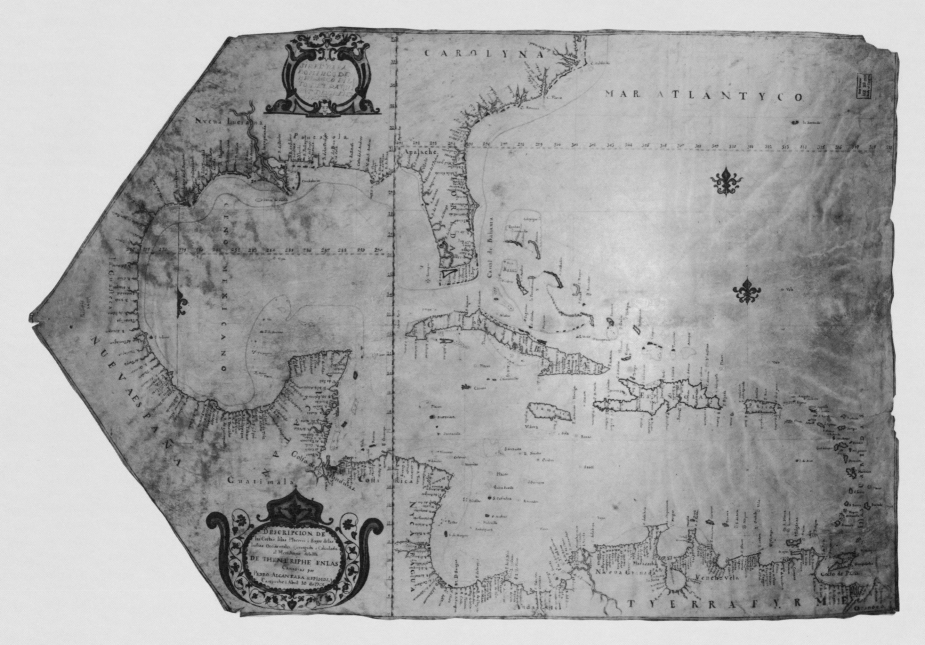

Manuscript chart of the Caribbean area, by Pedro A. Espinosa, Campeche, Mexico,
1765. Item no. 32.

parallel, apex to the left, 62.5 × 94 cm. Approximate scale 1:5,000,000.

The title, in the lower left corner, is enclosed within an ornately decorated and colored cartouche. In the upper left corner there is another decorated and colored cartouche with the following inscription: "Sirbe Para/Domingo De/Belasco Pilo/To Del Paqui/Bot Delrei El/Cortes."

The chart, which is neatly drawn in portolan style, includes the Gulf and southeastern Atlantic coasts of present United States, extending north beyond Cape Hatteras, the Gulf of Mexico and the bordering coasts of Mexico, the Caribbean Sea with the West Indies, and the bordering coasts of Central and South America. Latitude, with one-degree intervals, is indicated along a vertical line which extends from south to north on the left side of the chart. Longitude is indicated along two lines, one extending west from the latitude-designator across the Gulf of Mexico to the coast of Mexico and the second extending east from the latitude-designator, at approximately latitude 31 N., to the right (east) margin of the chart. As noted in the title, longitude is reckoned east from Tenerife Island in the Canaries. Faint rhumb lines radiate from major centers in the South Atlantic east of the Carolina coast, off the southeast tip of Hispaniola, and the western part of the Gulf of Mexico. There are numerous coastal names, most of which are written in portolan-style inward from the coast. Where space does not permit, names are written offshore. Lettering for Cuba and Española is in red, and initial letters for most other major names are in red. The balance of the lettering is black. There are two decorative and colored fleur-de-lis north-indicators in the Atlantic, and a half fleur-de-lis in the Gulf of Mexico. Several small holes in the corners of the chart suggest that it may have been at one time fastened to a board. Nothing is known about Pedro Alcantara Espinosa, and no other charts by him have been identified.

Within the neck area is the inscription "Phillipps MS 24996," indicating that, like no. 28, the Espinosa chart was at one time in the collection of Sir Thomas Phillipps. It was acquired by the Library of Congress in 1919. There is no record of a purchase price.

33

Caribbean, Gulf of Mexico, West Indies. [Cadiz?] ca. 1770 Anonymous (Spanish).

[Manuscript chart of the West Indies, Caribbean Sea, Gulf of Mexico, and bordering land areas of present southeastern United States, Mexico, Central America, and northern South America] Drawn on a sheet of vellum, trimmed evenly on the margins and on the simulated neck, which is to the left. A narrow elongation, 19 × 2.7 cm, extending from the simulated neck, was apparently designed to fasten the chart when rolled. 58 × 86 cm, exclusive of fastening strip. Approximate scale 1:6,000,000.

The chart is neatly drawn with black ink in portolan style. Coastal outlines and latitude and longitude indicators are in green. In area covered, cartographic style, and latitude and longitude indicators, this chart resembles the 1765 chart of Pedro Alcantara Espinosa (no. 32). As on no. 24, the name "Sⁿ Salbador" is applied to Eleuthera Island.

No. 33 was purchased in January 1928, from Maggs Brothers, London, in the same lot of material that included nos. 23, 24, 25, and 26. The reported purchase price for this chart was £12 10s.

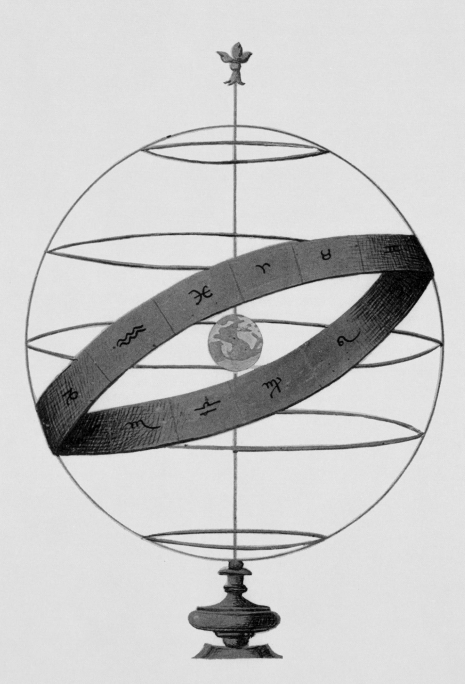

References

Almagià, Roberto. Intorno ad alcune carte nautiche Italiane conservate negli Stati Uniti. *In* Accademia Nazionale de Lincei. Atti, ser. 8, v. 7, fasc. 7–12, luglio/dic. 1952: 356–366.

————. Note intorno alla tradizione della cartografia nautico a Livorno. Rivista di Livorno, no. 5, 1950: 1–10.

————. Quelques questions au sujet des cartes nautiques et des portulans d'après les recherches récentes.
Reprint from *Archives internationales d'histoire des sciences*, no. 2, 1948: 237–246.

Andrews, Michael C. The boundary between Scotland and England in the portolan charts. *In* Society of Antiquaries of Scotland. Proceedings. v. 60; 1927. Edinburgh, 1927. p. 36–66.

————. The British Isles in the nautical charts of the XIVth and XVth centuries. Geographical journal, v. 68, 1926: 474–481.

Anthiaume, A. Cartes marines, constructions navales, voyages de découverte chez les Normands, 1500–1650. Paris, E. Dumont, 1916. 2 v. illus.

Bagrow, Leo. History of cartography. Rev. and enl. by R. A. Skelton. [English translation by D. L. Paisey] London, C. A. Watts, 1964.

Baltimore. *Museum of Art.* The world encompassed; an exhibition of the history of maps held at the Baltimore Museum of Art October 7 to November 23, 1952. Organized by the Peabody Institute Library, the Walters Art Gallery [and] the John Work Garrett Library of the Johns Hopkins University in cooperation with the Baltimore Museum of Art. Baltimore, Trustees of the Walters Art Gallery, 1952.

Bjørno, Axel A. Cartographica Groenlandica. Copenhagen, Reitzel, 1912.

Calegari, A. Carte nautiche eseguite in Livorno da Gio. Batta e Pietro Cavallini. Bollettino storico livornese, 1939: 200–205.

Campbell, Tony. The Drapers' Company and its school of seventeenth century chartmakers. *In* my head is a map; essays & memoirs in honour of R. V. Tooley, edited by Helen Wallis and Sarah J. Tyacke. London, Edwards, 1973.

Caraci, Giuseppe. Una carta nautica di Jaume Olives del 1557. L'Universo, v. 6, 1925: 23–26.

Champlain, Samuel de. The voyages and explorations of Samuel de Champlain, 1604–1616, narrated by himself. Translated by Annie Nettleton Bourne, together with the voyage of 1603, reprinted from Purchas his pilgrimes. Edited with introd. and notes by Edward Gaylord Bourne. New York, Allerton Book Co., 1922 [New York] AMS Press, 1973.

————. The works of Samuel de Champlain. Ed. by W. F. Ganong. Toronto, Champlain Society, 1922. (Champlain Society. Publications. [New series] v. 1)

Cortesão, Armando. Cartografia e cartógrafos portugueses dos séculos XV e XVI (Contribuïção par um estudo completo). Lisbõa, Edição de "Seara nova." 1935. 2 v. illus., maps.

————. History of Portuguese cartography. v. 1–2. Lisboa, Junta de Investigações do Ultramar, 1969–70. (Agrupamento de Estudos de Cartografia Antiga. Secção Anexa à Universidade de Coimbra. [Publicações] 6)

————. The nautical chart of 1424, and the early discovery and cartographical representtion of America. Coimbra, University of Coimbra, 1954.

————, and Avelino Teixeiro da Moto. Portugaliae monumenta cartographica. Lisboa, 1960. 5 v. and index volume.

Destombes, Marcel. Catalogue des cartes nautiques manuscrites sur parchemin, 1300–1700. Saigon, 1941.

Fischer, Theobald. Sammlung mittelalterlicher Welt- und Seekarten italienischen Ursprungs und aus italienischen Bibliotheken und Archiven. Vienna, F. Ongania, 1886.

Fite, Emerson D., and Archibald Freeman. A book of old maps delineating American history from the earliest days down to the close of the Revolutionary War. New York, Dover, 1969.
    Originally published in 1926 by Harvard University Press.

Garcia Camerero, Ernesto. La escuela cartográfica inglesa "at the Signe of the Platt." In Real Sociedad Geografica. Boletin. v. 95, 1959: 65–68.

Garcia Franco, Salvador. The "portolan mile" of Nordenskiöld. Imago mundi, no. 12, 1955: 89–91.

Gauld, George. An account of the surveys of Florida, &c., with directions for sailing from Jamaica or the West Indies, by the west end of Cuba, and through the Gulph of Florida. To accompany Mr. Gauld's charts. London, Faden, 1790.

Gernez, G. Les cartes avec échelle de latitudes auxiliare pour la région de Terre-Neuve. In L'Academie de Marine de Belgique. Communications. v. 11, 1952: 113.

Guillen y Tato, Julio. An unpublished atlas of J. Martinez (1591). Imago mundi, no. 12, 1965: 107–126.

Hamy, Jules E. T. Portolan charts of the XVth, XVIth, and XVIIth centuries collected by the late Theodore Jules Ernest Hamy. To be sold by auction Tuesday evening, November 19, 1912 . . . at the galleries of the Anderson Auction Company. [New York, 1912]

Hispanic Society of America. Facsimiles of portolan charts belonging to the Hispanic Society of America. Introduction by Edward Luther Stevenson. New York, 1916.

Howse, Derek, and Michael Sanderson. The sea chart. New York, McGraw-Hill, 1973.

International Geographical Union. Commission on Early Maps. Rapport au XVIIe Congrès international, Washington, 1952, par R. Almagià, President de la Commission. [Paris] 1952. 2 v.
    Contents: fasc. 1. Contributions pour un catalogue des cartes manuscrites, 1200–1500, éditées par M. Destombes (p. 1–20); Macrobius, par M. Destombes (p. 21–33); Richard de Haldingham, par G. R. Crone (p. 34–37); Cartes catalanes du XIVe siècle, par M. Destombes (p. 38–63). fasc. 2. Catalogue des cartes gravées au XVe siècle, par Marcel Destombes.

Kammerer, Albert. La découverte de la Chine par les Portugais au XVIème siècle et la cartographie des portulans. Avec des notes de toponymie chinoise, par Paul Pelliot. Leiden, E. J. Brill, 1944. (T'oung pao; archives concernant l'histoire, les langues, la géographie, l'ethnographie et les arts de l'Asie orientale. Suppl. au v. 39)

Kelley, J. E. A 15th century guide to weights and measures. Read at annual meeting, Society for the History of Discoveries, Washington, D.C., Nov. 1973. In press.

Kretschmer, Konrad. Die italienischen Portolane des Mittelalters; ein Beitrag zur Geschichte der Kartographie und Nautik. Hildesheim, G. Olms, 1962.
    Reprint of work originally published in 1909 by E. S. Mittler, Berlin.

La Guardia Trias, Rolando A. La aportación científica de Mallorquines y Portugueses a la cartografia náutica en los siglos XIV al XVI. [Madrid] Consejo Superior de Investigaciones Científicas, Instituto Histórico de Marina [1964].

Longhena, M. Atlanti e carte nautiche . . . conservati nella Biblioteca e nell'Archivio di Parma. Parma, 1907.

Lowery, Woodbury. A descriptive list of maps of the Spanish possessions within the present limits of the United States, 1502–1820. Ed. with notes by Philip Lee Phillips. Washington, Govt. Print. Off., 1912.

Martin, Lawrence, and Walter W. Ristow. A manuscript atlas by Battista Agnese. In Walter W. Ristow. A la carte; selected papers on maps and atlases. Washington, Library of Congress, 1972. p. 34–38.

Martines, Joan. Atlas de Joan Martínes, 1587. [Madrid, Ministerio de Education y Ciencia. Dirección General de Archivos y Bibliotecas, 1973]
    Facsimile edition.

Includes a "Prologo," i.e., introduction, by José Ibáñez Cerda, del Cuerpo de Archivos y Bibliotheca, which has biographical data about Joan Martines, and an inventory of nine charts and 18 atlases by him. The Library of Congress Martines atlas is not listed.

Newberry Library, *Chicago. Edward E. Ayer Collection.* List of manuscript maps in the Edward E. Ayer collection, comp. by Clara A. Smith, Chicago, 1927.
Includes descriptions of 10 portolan charts and 13 portolan atlases.

Nordenskiöld, Nils A. E. Periplus; an essay on the early history of charts and sailing directions; translated from the Swedish original by Francis A. Bather. Stockholm, Norstedt, 1897.
Reprint of 1967 is no. 52 in the Burt Franklin Research and Source Works Series.

Paris. Bibliothèque nationale. *Département des cartes et plans.* Catalogue des cartes nautiques sur vélin conservées au Département des cartes et plans. Par Myriem Foncin, Marcel Destombes, et Monique de la Roncière. Paris, Bibliothèque nationale, 1963.

Rey Pastor, Julio, *and* Ernesto García Camarero. La Cartografía mallorquina. Madrid, Consejo Superior de Investigaciones Científicas, 1960.

Ricci, Seymour de. Census of Medieval and Renaissance manuscripts in the United States and Canada. New York, Wilson, 1935–40. 3 v.
Suppl.: New York, Bibliographical Society of America, 1962.

Romans, Bernard. A concise history of East and West Florida. A facsimile reproduction of the 1775 edition with introduction by Rembert W. Patrick. Gainesville, University of Florida Press, 1962.

Rosenthal, Ludwig. Catalog. Munich, 1914.

Rüge, Walter. Aelteres kartographisches Material in deutschen Bibliotheken. Fünfter Bericht über die Jahre 1910–1913. *In* Gesellschaft der Wissenschaften zu Göttingen. *Philologisch-Historische Klasse.* Nachrichten. Beiheft 5, 1916: 1–28.

Smith, Thomas R. Manuscript and printed sea charts in seventeenth century London—the case of the Thames School. Los Angeles, University of California. (Clark lecture series) In press.

Spain. *Consejo Superior Geografico.* Cartografía histórica del cincuentenario. Atlas Catalán, 1375; carta de Juan de la Cosa, 1500. Madrid. 1974.
Text in Spanish, French, and English.

Stevenson, Edward Luther. Portolan charts, their origin and characteristics with a descriptive list of those belonging to the Hispanic Society of New York. New York, 1911.

Uzielli, Gustavo, *and* P. Amat de S. Filippo. Mappamondi, carte nautiche, portolani ed altri monumenti cartografici specialmente italiani dei secoli XIII–XVII. Amsterdam, Meridian Pub. Co., 1967.
Unabridged reprint of *Studi biografici e bibliografici sulla storia della geografia in Italia,* v. 2, 2d ed. (Roma, 1882)

Voorbeijtel Cannenburg, Willem. A Dutch chart that survived the ages. Imago mundi, no. 4, 1948: 63.

Wagner, Henry R. The manuscript atlases of Battista Agnese. *In* Bibliographical Society of America. Papers, v. 21, 1931: 1–110.

———. Additions to the manuscript atlases of Battista Agnese. Imago mundi, no. 4, 1947: 28–30.

Winsor, Justin. Baptista Agnese and American cartography in the 16th century. *In* Massachusetts Historical Society. Proceedings. 2d ser., v. 11; 1896–97. Boston, 1897. p. 372–385.

Winter, Heinrich. Catalan portolan maps and their place in the total view of cartographic development. Imago mundi, no. 11, 1954: 1–12.

———. The origin of the sea chart. Omago mundi. no. 13, 1956: 39–44.

Yūsuf Kamāl, Prince. Hallucinations scientifiques (les portulans). Leiden, E. J. Brill, 1937.

☆ U.S. GOVERNMENT PRINTING OFFICE : 1977 O—588-333

For sale by the Superintendent of Documents, U.S. Government Printing Office
Washington, D.C. 20402

Stock No. 030-004-00016-7